P237/X

The

Dead Sea

Scrolls

By THEODORE HELINE

DeVorss and Company, *Publishers*
P.O. Box 550
Marina del Rey, CA 90291

Charlotte Carter

First Edition, 1957

Eighth Edition, 1980

3/99

PREFACE TO THE FOURTH EDITION – 1970

Several years have passed since the previous edition of this work on the Scrolls was published. In that interval the Dead Sead Scrolls have increased in number and have been enriched by continued deciphering and interpretations. It could not have been otherwise considering the wide interest and great significance of the subject, since the Scrolls contain the most important and authentic records in existence of the spiritual community that became the divinely inspired agency for uniting the enduring values of the Hebrew scriptures with that of the emerging Christian revelation.

This placed them in a position from which they were able, by teachings and practices, to preserve for posterity a record of that which was transpiring spiritually in the century when there were no more prophets in Israel and when the Christian gospels had not yet been written. Thus the Scrolls are so intimately related to our Scriptures, Old and New, that they will ever seem as though a very part of the Bible itself. These priceless Essenian documents, both sacred and secular, are charged with life; they reveal directly and indirectly the unfoldment in history through human instrument, divine plan and purpose. So interest in the Scrolls, and their contents, as subjects for study and meditation will never die.

Nothing spectacular in connection with the Scrolls has come to light in the past decade or so. For the most part the studies have upheld all major findings and conclusions of the earlier years. This is brought out at length in a volume published in 1969 by the Oxford University Press and authored by Edmund Wilson. It will be remembered that it was in an article in The New Yorker in 1955 by this same writer that the discovery of the Scrolls was first introduced through a popular news medium to a wide reading public and aroused an interest in the subject that went far beyond its religious and archeological aspects. In that article Mr. Wilson predicted that the ultimate importance of the Scrolls would lie in their proof that Jesus, the New Testament and early Christianity came of Jewry, and that these documents from the first century B.C. and the first century A.D. would precipitate a new era in biblical studies. And so they have.

Among the new discoveries enumerated by Mr. Wilson are two copper scrolls containing an inventory of buried treasure, which may or may not have been temple objects hidden from the Romans in 68 A.D.; an Aramaic version of Genesis, somewhat different from the biblical version; a new manuscript of the Psalms, and a commentary on the Psalms and the Prophets.

Then there is a chapter describing Herod's fortress and palace where the Zealots, a sect that was closely related to the Essenes, made their last stand against the invading Romans. A dramatic account is given of the Zealots' hopeless position. Knowing that they could not possibly hold out against the mighty forces of their assailants, rather than surrender they committed mass suicide.

Also of very special interest is the uncovering of "The Mysterious 151st Psalm." This Psalm is not in our Bible as we have it, but it was previously known as having been included in the Septuagint, the Greek version of the Old Testament. The reason for the omission of this Psalm is not definitely known but conjecture has it that it was probably due to supposed Greek Orphic influence. Not by inference of any kind was David "the sweet singer of Israel with his harp," to share with Orpheus and his lyre the glory of producing music of such magic as to bring a lively response from nature itself. Such it was that the trees sang in unison with the harpist's chords, and flocks in the fields stood still and spellbound. One can but observe that sectarianism can cut deeply into Realities that are Whole.

The long-buried Scrolls have been resurrected. What they relate of the past is interesting; what they have to say to the present is important. The historical period in which they came into being corresponds in its deeper aspects to what is happening in our time. The Essenes of the Scrolls piloted the ship of State, Palestine, and its extended areas of influence, in its passage from the Hebrew Dispensation into the Christian. It pointed the way from the passing Zodiacal Age of Aries into that of the emerging Age of Pices.

Today we have a like passage to negotiate, namely, that of a declining Piscean influence into that of an increasing Aquarian way of life. This passage entails dangers and difficulties, trials and tribulations, challenges and perplexities. But it also holds for us high hopes, great promise, glorious victories. The Forces of Light are emerging from out of a shadowed world with unprecedented radiance. They are here, and ours to the grasp. The issues to be met are basically of a spiritual nature as they were in the time of Christ. The Essenes knew this and acted upon it. They won out; they fulfilled their divine calling.

We too shall win by laying hold of what was fundamental in the way of this ancient Brotherhood of the White Raiment. The ideals they resolved to live by, the virtues they cultivated, the principles they adhered to and the unfaltering faith in Divine Guidance by which they governed their individual and collective lives are as binding upon the way of true progress today as they were two thousand years ago. Their validity, being of the spirit, is timeless.

There are many reincarnated Essenes in our world today. They have come to help in another transitional period in the world's history. Some of these returnees have conscious remembrance of their former relationship, while others are aware of it through soul impressions that they have come to recognize as authentic by the natural impulses that lead them to follow in the main the Essene pattern and to work selflessly for the attainment of like objectives. Such make up scattered present-day groups united in purpose and dedication. From their past experience they have developed qualifications that enable them to spearhead the valiant forerunners that are out to explore at all costs a new kind of world. This is not motivated by self interest; it springs from the High Self in its love for humanity. It is for the less-awakened masses that they willingly and joyously perform a sacrificial service.; They are renunciates who have already found the Kingdom of God on earth. Their number is relatively small but their influence is great.

A community of Essenes residing in Palestine and adjacent areas presided over the transition period of two thousand years ago. Their spiritual offspring is now to be found in numerous small communes all over the world. Members composing some of these groups may never have heard of the Essenes but have been magnetically drawn together in response to the same God-given guidance and inspiration that brought the Essene community into being. This appears from the fact that their approach to the problems to be solved is like that of their spiritual forebears. They follow the same general line of conduct, practices and disciplines. They are in the world but not of it. They are a people apart from the established order. This withdrawal is not in order to escape from responsibilities but to better their condition for doing more for their fellowman than would otherwise be possible. They are John the Baptists out of the "wilderness," crying out in a voice to be heard that the hour has struck for making way for a life more meaningful and abundant than that which prevailing self-indulgent living and materialistic objectives can provide.

To point up how this movement is activated into the living, throbbing forceful present, Life Magazine in 1969 issue described and illustrated certain communes springing up here and there that are dedicated to finding their way into a fresher, clearer, and more natural and joyous life by moving out into the open and relating themselves more closely and creatively with Nature and Nature's God. Unfortunately all communes do not fall within this category.

All this serves to underline the fact that the more familiar we become with what the Scrolls have to teach us, not just to satisfy an intellectual curiosity as to what happened centuries ago, but for study and meditation on the principles, practices and beliefs they set forth, we shall be the better equipped to move successfully into a New Order of the Ages.

The Essenes of yesterday made straight the way for the first coming of the Christ. It is for their spiritual forebears of today to do the same for His second coming.

*The most important teaching man has received
to aid him in the understanding of the
Christ Event had its source in these
(Theraputae and Essene) communities.*

—Rudolf Steiner

*There is hope for that
which is moulded in clay
to have converse with things
everlasting.*

—From an Essene Psalm

CONTENTS

PART ONE

THE DEAD SEA SCROLLS

PART TWO

THE SCROLLS SEVERALLY CONSIDERED

PART THREE

FORERUNNERS – PAST AND PRESENT

THE
DEAD SEA
SCROLLS

THE ESSENIAN
FORERUNNERS OF CHRIST

by
Theodore Heline

PART ONE

THE DEAD SEA SCROLLS

Their Bearing on the Essenian
Forerunners of the Christ

ith the recent discovery of those ancient Palestinian records that have come to be known as *The Dead Sea Scrolls*, important facts bearing on the birth of Christianity have arrested the attention not only of scholars and Biblical students, but of the reading and thinking public at large. This general interest in their content signals their discovery as an event of very special significance.

The scrolls are remnants of a library belonging to the Essenes, a religious sect that founded a settlement in the Judean hills near the Dead Sea sometime in the second century before Christ. At a place called Qumran a Bedouin shepherd, searching for a lost goat, entered a cave and came upon the greatest documentary find in all history. That was in 1947. Since then continued explorations of other nearby caves have yielded treasure upon treasure numbering hundreds of manuscripts. Most of them are mere fragments but of very great importance since they include portions of nearly every book of the Old Testament together with apocryphal works, hymns and writings about the Essenes. Many of these Biblical manuscripts antedate the traditional Hebrew text underlying our English Bible by more than a thousand years.

There are nine caves clustering around the ancient Essene center; in these the priceless manuscripts have been found. Some

3

of them are of leather, others are done on papyrus, still others are copper rolls. The first cave held the great *Isaiah* scroll, almost a complete version of this Biblical book, also *A Commentary on the Book of Habakkuk*, a previously unknown work, and the Essene *Manual of Discipline*, as it has been called. Much of the foregoing material has been published in English and in Hebrew. The latter was done by the Hebrew University in Jerusalem and contains, besides the major items, a second *Isaiah Scroll*, a sectarian psalter and an Essene account of the *War of the Sons of Light.*

The next important discovery was in the fourth cave, from which more than three hundred manuscripts were removed. Unlike those found in the first cave which were preserved in sealed earthen jars, these were quite unprotected from the elements and so in a more or less fragmentary condition. The explorations continue. According to reports, these have now extended into nearly three hundred neighboring caves. And as the search goes on each year adds to the discoveries.

The first lot of scrolls offered for sale by the Bedouins was acquired by the Syrian head of St. Mark's Monastery in Jerusalem. Six months later another lot was sold to the Hebrew University, also in Jerusalem. By 1955 the St. Mark's scrolls were sold to an American who presented them to the Israeli government. Together with other ancient documents, they were now to be housed in a Jerusalem museum built by the government for this special purpose, to be called "The Shrine of the Books." All the scrolls have been made available to the American School of Oriental Research in Jerusalem.

A number of other scrolls, including some inscribed on copper, are owned by the government of Jordan but were loaned for a time to the University of Manchester in England. In 1954 McGill University of Montreal purchased some manuscript fragments for $15,000. Then in 1956 others came into the possession of McCormick Theological Seminary in Chicago, at a reputed cost of $75,000. The purchase was made from Bedouins through the offices of the Jordan government. Undoubtedly there are still more manuscripts in Arabian hands awaiting the light of day as competitive bidding for these literary treasures mounts higher and higher.

The work of deciphering, translating, collating and interpreting all this material is a task that will absorb scholars for many years to come. A concordance covering five of the scrolls has already been prepared by the aid of the mechanical brain of a gigantic data processing machine.

Scroll Studies

Perhaps the most popular of early presentations on the subject of the scrolls was a lengthy article by Edmund Wilson in *The New Yorker*, May 14, 1955. As everyone knows, this is not the type of magazine one looks to for serious studies in history, archeology, religion and the like. But here was an effective medium for reaching a wide public with something that was not merely an absorbing story of a thrilling discovery and an event of genuine historic significance, but a recital that led the reader on into meaningful reflections about the very spiritual and cultural foundations on which our Western Christian civilization has been built.

Such cognitions are important at our present point in history when we must recapitulate the type of work done by the Essenes and their associates two thousand and more years ago. As they helped at that time to prepare new foundations for the Piscean Age that was then dawning—and which is now drawing toward its close—so must we today help lay new foundations for the Aquarian Age that lies ahead. Matters pertaining to such developments are, therefore, not just a concern of scholars and specialists. They are for everyone's consideration. When a culture or civilization is transiting from one definite stage or phase into another, as is the case in our time, it is important that people understand not only what is taking place, but also what can be done to accelerate the process. Familiarity with *The Dead Sea Scrolls* and their outraying implications can well become a helpful contributary factor to this end.

An extensive literature has now developed around the scrolls. Hundreds of articles have appeared in religious and scientific magazines, and also in more popular media. There are many books on the subject. A series of volumes are now in process of publication by the Oxford University Press. Among those addressed to laymen and that have reached a large reading public may be mentioned the volume on the scrolls by Mr. Wilson, which is an amplification of the article published in *The New Yorker*. In 1952 A. Dupont-Sommer, Professor of Semitic Languages at the Sorbonne in Paris, published what he called a "preliminary survey" of the scrolls which was made available promptly in English translation. By 1955 this first edition had grown to twice its original size and its title was also doubled. The first was titled simply, *The Dead Sea Scrolls*; the second, *The Jewish Sect of Qumram and the Essenes—New Studies on the Dead Sea Scrolls*. This shift of emphasis from the scrolls to the people of the scrolls, as indicated by the change in title, is especially interesting to our own particular approach to the subject. To Dupont-Sommer goes credit for being the first public champion to identify the Dead Sea Community with the Essenes.

In 1955 Millar Burrows, Professor of Biblical Theology at Yale University, brought out a four-hundred-page volume which, he states, "is not intended for the scholar" but was written "with a man's pen, so that he who runs may read." He has evidently succeeded since the volume in hand indicates that five months after publication it was in its seventh printing.

As a further indication of the widespread interest in the scrolls it may be noted that the bibliography of magazine articles contained in Mr. Burrows' volume runs to sixteen pages, and these include only a "selected" list of highly specialized periodicals. Material to be found in the popular magazines on the one hand, and in the more restricted field of occultism on the other, is entirely omitted; nor is mention made of the attention devoted to the subject by the daily press. An interesting feature of Mr. Burrows' bibliography is the preponderance of French and German items. There are whole pages with scarcely an English reference in them.

Mention may also be made of two more studies. These appeared in 1956, both of them addressed to the general reader. One is *The*

Dead Sea Scriptures by Theodor H. Gaster; the other, *The Dead Sea Scrolls and the Originality of Christ* by Geoffrey Graystone. The first is dedicated "To the Memory of the Men of Qumram." It gives a complete translation of the principal scrolls together with notes, but in the words of the author, "it does not venture into any detailed discussion of the various theories that have been advanced concerning their date, the possibility of recognizing historical allusions, and the like." It is "concerned only with what the Scrolls themselves have to say, and not with what has been or is being said about them."

The second of the two works is a small volume containing reprints of articles that first appeared in the *Irish Theological Quarterly*. It has two objectives: one, to consider the light which the scrolls shed on the background of New Testament times, and the problem of their possible influence on sacred writers and early Christianity generally; second, to stress "the originality of Christ" and the independent ground on which His ministry and teaching proceeded. The text is clear, concise, comprehensive. It emanates from "Rome," literally and theologically, and is apparently representative of the position which Catholic scholars have taken in regard to the scrolls. In emphasizing the uniqueness of the Christ Event, there is, according to our evaluation, an underrating of the antecedent developments that did so much to bring that Event to pass. This, from our point of view, is at once its chief virtue and its one shortcoming. The incomparable position occupied by the Christ in the spiritual life of the race enhances rather than diminishes the significance of all that entered into the preparation for His taking on flesh and dwelling among us. The Divine Incarnation did not require an annulment of the historical process; it utilized it in a manner and to a degree unequalled either before or since. It is thoughts such as these that the information contained in the scrolls tends to strengthen and clarify.

Biblical and Sectarian Scrolls

Theological scholars and Bible students are likely to be especially interested in the Biblical scrolls. They conform so closely to accepted texts that they strengthen confidence in the integrity of the current Old Testament version, thus confusing critics who maintain there have been so many changes in the course of the centuries due to mistranslations, faulty transmissions and actual surreptitious interpolations that the Scriptures we have today are not to be taken too seriously as a body of "divine revelation." To be sure, the human hand is there with all its slips, errors and wilful changes, but from this it must not be concluded that our Holy Scriptures are a fortuitous collection of writings devoid of an overriding spiritual design. There is both an artistic and a scientific pattern discoverable in both the Old and the New Testaments that were certainly not present in the minds of either Biblical scribes or collaters, but to which all were in the main responsive. Such conclusions are substantially fortified in the discovery of scrolls which contain versions of parts of the Old Testament that are some ten centuries older than any previously known, and which, while they contain many minor variations, have no major departures from the long accepted texts. Biblical exegesists, working with letter, word and verse, will have many revisions to make. But if one's faith in divine revelation rests on the spirit radiating out from the whole and not on spellings, constructions and the like, it is safe to say that if the whole of the Old Testament were uncovered in the completeness with which we now have Isaiah, for example, the wonder would be how it could have maintained its basic structure through the many vicissitudes it has encountered in the course of millennia.

To esoteric students the literature of the Essenes is of the greatest interest. This is true for more than one reason. The Essenes were the esotericists of their time. They were among the chief custodians of the Mystery Teachings of old. They possessed literature they were permitted to "show only to the wise." To their hands was entrusted the sacred books of Israel committed to writing by Ezra (Esdras) in the mystic Field of Ardath at Babylon several hundred years previously. They were thus the link between the Old and the New Dispensations, the divinely commissioned forerunners of the Christ and the illumined heralds of a new gospel. It is a thrilling discovery that brings this saintly society

8

into a clearer light than has been shed upon it since the days of the early Christian community.

Judaism's Three Sects

The Essenes, the Pharisees and the Sadducees were the three principal sects within Judaism in Christ's time. The Essenes were, in the words of Madam Blavatsky, "the religionists of the new faith." They were strictly an esoteric society. The Sadducees were the priestly class, which had lost the inner light through overabsorption in material interests. They believed neither in angels nor the immortality of the soul, so might be designated the religious materialists of their day. The Pharisees were recruited from among scribes, lawyers and interpreters of the law. They were so attached to its letter that they lost sight of its spirit In other words, they were the traditionalists.

And so neither the Sadducees nor the Pharisees were able to read aright the signs of their times. They knew the law and the prophets. They taught the coming of a world redeemer. Still they were unable to recognize the actual preparation being made by the Essenes for receiving Him. Lacking spiritual perception, they not only failed to recognize their Messiah when He came but they became His enemies. They crucified Him. Thus tragically did they miss their mission. For they were the official leaders of Israel whose national and racial destiny it was to provide a physical vehicle in the person of Jesus of Nazareth for the Divine Incarnation and to establish a suitable environment and community atmosphere for His manifestation and ministry. In all of this they failed.

But the redemptive plan of the ages was not to be frustrated by the failure of men even if it be those called to be in the forefront of its fulfillment. In the background were souls who had not lost the inner light and who had kept faith with the Mystery Wisdom. They had girded themselves by spiritual disciplines to make straight the way for the coming One. These were the Essenes.

In order to keep themselves unspotted by the world they withdrew from town and city to the desert, where they formed themselves into a closed community dedicated to the cultivation of a spiritual life. This withdrawal was not motivated by selfishness. It was not done to evade their responsibilities to the larger national community to which they belonged. On the contrary, it was motivated by a deep and genuine selflessness. They envisioned a world in need and took it upon themselves to create conditions that would meet the requirements of the Messiah who was to become the world's Savior. It was a sacrificial movement which they undertook. It entailed the strictest disciplines, an ascetic way of life, and virtual ostracism by the conventional world about them. They were different, too different, to mingle freely with the throngs and to follow their manner of living.

The Essenes called themselves the New Israel. They also regarded themselves as the people of the New Testament. The terms have like significance. Old Israel was the people of the Old Testament. The time had come for the Old Dispensation to give way to the New. The Essenes were alive to the transition under way and so made it their special mission to understand its demands and to serve its needs.

The "Silent" Centuries Speak

One of the scholars working on the scrolls, W. F. Albright of John Hopkins University, says *The Dead Sea Scrolls* are "unquestionably the most valuable of all scrolls yet known from the standpoint of history." They fill in a goodly portion of the four centuries that elapsed between the Old and New Dispensations, a period which has been referred to as the "silent" centuries. Now that silence has been dramatically broken by the discovery of the scrolls.

These ancient documents, assigned to a period from about 200 B.C. to 70 A.D., contribute not only fresh and important information about the thinking and practices of the immediate successors of the Hebrew prophets but also inspirational writings that perpetuate the prophetic office of the ancient seers of Israel together with records indicating their dedication to the task of

10

fulfilling Isaiah's injunction, "Prepare ye the way of the Lord, make straight in the desert a highway for our God."

This is precisely what the people of the scrolls did. Seven hundred years after Isaiah's call to action, these words of the "Evangelical Prophet," as he has been called, were voiced again by the Evangelist Matthew in the opening Book of the New Testament, wherein he tells of John the Baptist preaching in the wilderness of Judea the Kingdom of God with the same fervor as did Isaiah before him, and echoing his very words, "Prepare ye the way of the Lord, make his paths straight."

John the Baptist belonged to the company that linked the Old Dispensation to the New. He was an Essene, and the scene of his labors was in the desert of Judea in the vicinity of the Dead Sea, where the monastery of the brotherhood to which he belonged was situated. It was in this same region by the Jordan that he baptized Jesus, an individual initiatory act which sprang naturally from the prescribed ritual bathing practiced by the Essenes. It was not a Jewish rite but a sacramental ceremony that later became a part of the sacred ordinances of the Christian church. The same was true of the Essenian practice of partaking of bread and wine at their communal meals before this act was solemnized at the Last Supper.

In the period with which we are dealing, official Judaism, as previously noted, was in the hands of traditionalists and a selfcentered priesthood. The Sadducees, a term meaning the sons of Zadok, were the priestly caste. Zadok was the High Priest under David and the first of the Jewish priestly line to serve in the Temple of Solomon. But the Sadducees were no longer true to their trust. Selfish interests vied with priestly service. Traders were permitted to carry on their transactions in holy places, a sacrilege that moved the Christ to expel the money changers from the Temple.

But the priestly calling was not to be abandoned. It was to be restored to its rightful place of honor and to be kept worthy of presiding at the altar of the Lord. Qualifications for such service rested primarily, not on physical inheritance but on spiritual fitness. This priestly qualification the Essenes sought to fulfill in

11

their lives. Hence they called themselves the Sons of Zadok, a designation they claimed by spiritual lineage, not according to physical descent. The hereditary priesthood had commenced to give way to an elected priesthood, a priesthood recruited through Initiation.

In this connection there is a statement about the Essenes by Josephus, the Jewish historian of the first century of our Era, to the effect that the binding element in their community life was not based on blood ties but on their zeal for virtue and their love of mankind. Nothing of greater significance could be said of the Essenes than just this. It places them definitely on the side of the New Dispensation. They were, in this respect as in many others, Christians before Christ's coming.

Transcending the Blood Bond

The blood tie was the basis of brotherhood in the Old Dispensation. Social unities were determined by physical relationship. Excepting the Essenes, pre-Christian Hebrews, even as the Jews to this day, were banded together by virtue of their common descent from Father Abraham. The Christ came to loosen that blood bond and replace it by one of the spirit. Said the Christ in effect to the Jews who prided themselves on being the elect because they were children of Abraham, "Before Abraham was, I Am." By this statement He was directing His hearers to a higher inheritance, an inheritance from God the Father. This inheritance, being common to all humanity, makes all men brothers. The Essenes had not merely accepted this fact intellectually, they lived it. Hence they were motivated primarily not by hereditary impulses that flowed in their blood but by promptings that arose from within the egoic center of their being. They had already contacted the Cosmic Ego, the Christ, before His incarnation and attuned their life to His. They had thus transcended separative racial thinking and become true universalists.

It is the destiny of all humanity to one day achieve this liberation from limiting racial ties and to come into a living realization of the oneness of mankind. At the very heart of the mission of Christ lies the need to assist humanity to attain this state. This assistance was not rendered once and for all at the time of His earthly sojourn; it is a continuing ministry. From inner worlds He continues to radiate into our human sphere impulses that strengthen the egoic life of man, awakening within him a recognition of his spiritual selfhood and immortal destiny as a son of God.

That the Essenes had made conscious contact with the Cosmic Christ, for whose imminent incarnation they were making most careful preparation, is evident from their writings which at many points parallel what the writers of the Gospels were able to record after their personal association with Christ Jesus. For example, the Essene *Manual of Discipline*, one of the most important of the newly discovered manuscripts, contains a statement almost identical with that with which Saint John opens his Gospel. The Essene reading is as follows, "And by his knowledge everything has been brought into being. And everything that is, he established by his purpose apart from him nothing is done." John's version of this same sublime truth, so familiar to every Christian, reads, "The same was in the beginning with God. All things were made by him and without him was not anything made that was made." Such profound statements could arise only out of Initiate consciousness. St. John possessed it, as is evidenced by his Gospel. The Essenes before him possessed it, as evidenced by their writings.

Essenian Universalism

Since the Essenian forerunners of the Christ had transcended barriers that divide classes, races and religions, their spiritual philosophy was sufficiently universal and cosmic for them to incorporate into their own indigenous religious system the best elements of most closely related cultures, which embraced the Grecian, Persian and Egyptian. One of their principal centers was at Alexandria in Egypt. There they were known as the Therapeutae. Pythagoras was highly venerated among them and

13

Zoroaster lived again in teachings that were central to the spiritual purpose they had come to serve.

Zoroaster proclaimed the coming of the Great Sun Spirit whom we call the Christ. He directed his followers to contemplate the Cosmic Being that shone within the radiant physical Sun, the Being of Light, the effulgent Solar Aura, the Ahura Mazda which, he declared, was drawing closer to the earth and that the time would come when this cosmic Individuality would take on human form and become the light of the world. It was the teaching echoed by Saint John as he bears witness to the Word, the Logos, the Solar Logos, that became flesh and dwelt among us. It was the same Being who, according to the Gospel records, declared of Himself that He was Light of the World.

"The Essenes revered the sun," writes Albert Pike in his monumental Masonic work, *Morals and Dogmas*, "not as a god but as a symbol of light and fire; the fountain of which the Orientals supposed God to be." Hence the great solar festivals of the solstices were observed by them "in a distinguished manner."

In keeping with this reverence for the solar orb as the habitation of the Light of the World, the rising and setting of the Sun were greeted with hymns of praise and marked times of observing certain sacred ceremonials. Also, in their devotions they turned toward the rising sun. It was a rule among them not to use the power of the spoken word before sunrise unless it pertained to holy matters.

The Essenes perpetuated the Zoroastrian teachings dealing with the conflict between the powers of light and of darkness. Ormuzd stood at the head of the Forces of Light while Ahriman, whom we call the Adversary, championed the Powers of Darkness or materiality. The title given to one of the Essene manuscripts included in *The Dead Sea Scrolls* is, as previously noted, *The War of the Sons of Light*, or in a lengthier title, *The War of the Children of Light Against the Children of Darkness*.

In this connection Albert Pike observes that while the Essenes were less distinguished by metaphysical speculation than by simple meditation and moral practice, their teaching partook of the Zoroastrian principle that it was necessary to free the soul from

14

the trammels and influences of matter. This conviction led them to the adoption of their ascetic way of life.

Thus we may observe again and again how the spiritual stream of diving revelation flows on through the centuries and the ages. The channel is not always equally broad and deep; nor is it always straight. But on and on it flows through time, ever increasing in volume as it winds its way toward the ocean of light in which it will one day lose itself, only to find its completion by identification with the Divine Whole.

There are no abrupt breaks in the evolutionary process. There are times when events long in process of development burst into fruition. So it was in the life of mankind when the Christ descended to earth in the form of a man. An event came to pass according to a plan that had been steadily unfolding for ages. All the preChristian religions participated in that plan. The Essenes literally presided over its actual culmination.

Belated Recognition

That the Essenes were well known for their high idealism and spiritual influence appears in testimonies of such eminent contemporaries as Josephus; Pliny the Elder, the Roman observer; and Philo, the Jewish Hellenistic philosopher of Alexandria. All agree in ascribing the highest virtues to this apocalyptic sect. Pliny referred to them as "the most extraordinary people in the world." Josephus declared that they surpassed both the Greeks and Barbarians in virtue and succeeded in maintaining a high level of discipline. Philo, like Josephus, stated that they were brought together by love of their fellow man and not through Jewish blood. In support of this statement he said that wherever they established a center, they appointed one of their number to welcome strangers and look out for their guest's needs. All sick and elderly persons were cared for; widows and orphans and those in trouble became their concern; and, in respect to their common humanity, they regarded all as brothers regardless of station or condition in life. As of the spirit there was equality.

According to the records, Josephus once tried to join the

brotherhood but apparently he either failed to qualify or did not wish to meet the severe requirements for admission into its inner circle.

With such high ratings given the Essenes by their illustrious contemporaries, questions naturally arise as to why they have not entered more prominently into historical records and, more especially, why they were not better known among Christians since they were in deed and in truth among the founding fathers of the Christian faith. How could it be that this community that called itself the people of the New Dispensation are never once mentioned in the Gospels or any other writings of the New Testament? How could they have been left out of Scriptures which took form in their midst and incorporated much of their very own teachings and practices? Several considerations enter into answers to these questions.

The Essenes were not in the forefront of the external affairs of their time. In the social, religious, political and economic activities of their day they were in the background. They were a minority group. They are said to have numbered about four to five thousand. They abstained from prominent participation in world affairs in order to serve more effectively the inconspicuous but supremely important spiritual requirements of their destiny, namely, making preparations for the coming of the Christ. That they might cultivate their spiritually superior way of life, they sought out secluded places for their habitation. They were by-passed by the crowd until their leader, sometimes referred to as the Master of Justice, commenced to exercise an influence that tended to seriously disturb the established order. Then it was that they became the object of persecution, their leader being condemned and put to death. The Essenes were keyed to a higher standard of life than were average individuals because they belonged more to the future than to their own period.

As an organized movement the Essenes disappeared from history at an early date, being absorbed by the early Church. After this they became known as Christians. Their name changed but not their character, their inner vision or their dedication to serve the Lord of Light. No single community of believers did more to verify the general observation made by the early Church Father, St. Augustine, when he averred that what we now call the Christian religion "really was known to the ancients, nor was wanting at any time from the beginning of the human race, until the time when Christ came in the flesh; from whence the true religion, which had previously existed, began to be called Christian..."

Certain it is that the Essenes were not left unmentioned in the New Testament because its authors were unaware of either their presence or the profound influence they exercised in the preparation of the events they recorded and in formulation of the faith they expounded. On the contrary, the omission of their name from pages of the new Scriptures was due to the fact that they themselves were at the very heart of producing those sacred writings. They entered into it. What they did and taught was woven into the very texture of the Christian Scriptures. "It is clear," writes Frank M. Cross, Jr., in a series of articles based on his own scholarly studies of the scrolls, which appeared in the August 1955 issues of *The Christian Century*, "that reworked Essene documents were published in the early Christian community; *Enoch*, the *Testaments of the Twelve Patriarchs*, and perhaps the *Assumption of Moses*. The doctrine of the *Two Ways*, Essene formulations found in the *Didache* (Teaching of the Twelve Apostles) and the *Epistle of Barnabas* . . . make clear that direct use of Essene materials was made in the Christian composition."

It was otherwise with the Pharisees and Sadducees. They were creating no new literature. They were suspicious of anything that did not echo the old. They presided over the conventional religionists of their day. They were the comfortable, well-established and self-righteous sects. They entered into the New Testament only externally, as it were, whereas the Essenes were were internally a part of it. The Pharisees and Sadducees constituted the opposition; the Essenes, the supporters of the Christ in channeling a new energizing and transforming power into the life of humanity. As previously observed, it was inability on the part of established sectarian leaders to recognize the light that shone in their darkness, and their failure to measure up to the task that was theirs by virtue of the spiritual offices they held, that drew the censure directed against them by the Christ and by which alone they enter into scriptural records. They became parties to the crucifixion of Him whom they were meant to exalt. This it was that earned them the unenviable immortality of being inscribed upon pages of the New Testament.

Now, after two thousand years, the Essenes who were in the background of world attention in their own time—though at the very heart of the Event that continues to reshape the world—are emerging in their true importance as the light of the New Day falls upon the contribution they made to the spiritual evolution of humanity at the supreme historic moment of all time.

Forerunners by Merit

The distinction of fulfilling so important a mission at the time of Christ's advent did not come to the Essenes by chance; it came to them because of merit. This band of forerunners was composed of old souls, enlightened men and women, consecrated individuals, many of them disciples and Initiates of high degree. They had come together in time and place to perform the most glorious task ever given to man, namely, cradling the Christ child and nucleating the Christian faith. Election to this office came from neither leaders nor populace of their land and age. It was by ordination on a higher plane and was bestowed, not with the concurrence of contemporary religionists, but in spite of the latter's active opposition and actual persecution.

The opportunity of creating and maintaining a spiritually charged center on the face of the earth, a center into which the Anointed One could descend and make Himself manifest, came to a relatively small group that had attained consciousness of the Christ. They were not merely to announce His coming but were to surround and protect His very presence. This they did for the Child Jesus, for the developing Nazarine youth, and later for the Christed Jesus as He carried out His three-year earthly ministry.

They also exercised special care over Joseph and Mary and protected them during their flight into Egypt. They helped the

Disciples and early evangelizers who went forth without purse or scrip to preach the new gospel. Their sphere of action was not limited to their monastic community by the Dead Sea but extended throughout Palestine. So-called "cells" were formed in villages; from them they seeded the ground for a Christed harvest.

Brethren of this esoteric fraternity were active in Egypt, Greece and related territories. They did not always or everywhere bear the same name. According to Pliny they were a hermetic society that had existed from ages past. In the Book of Judges, composed a thousand years before the Christian era, this same esoteric body is referred to as Nazarines. In the Book of Kings they are designated as the School of the Prophets. At a later date the Book of Maccabees speaks of them as an inner circle that was not only singularly "devoted to the law" but also manifested to a high degree the "active love of God." They were contemporaries of the Essenes and apparently related to the latter, not by any outer groupings but rather by what they held in common esoterically and, above all, in their response to the solar Love Ray that was approaching the earth prior to actual Incarnation. Being among the forerunners of the Lord of Love, they were exhibiting faithful obedience to the Law and a growing awareness of the truth expressed in Paul's words to the Romans, "love is the fulfilling of the law."

The Pythagoreans of Greece, of whom we shall have more to say, had much in common with the Essenes, as did the Therapeutae of Egypt. The latter were adept at healing—therapists, as the name indicates. "It is evident," writes Madame Blavatsky in *Isis Unveiled*, "that Philo's Therapeutes are a branch of the Essenes. Their name indicates it—*Esseion* (Greek), asaya, physician." To which she adds, "Luke, who was a physician, is designated in the Syriac texts as Asaia, the Essenian or Essene." To heal, to serve, to worship, these were the ideals guiding every activity of the members of these differently designated but like-minded and similarly-dedicated communities, even as they characterized their direct and immediate successors, the early Christians. This unity of spirit, this bond of brotherhood which existed between the esoteric groups that functioned both before

19

and after the coming of Christ, is based on their common contact with the Divine Gnosis. It rests on a revelation of the Arcane Mysteries.

Religion's Historical Continuity

The unfoldment of the Divine Plan for man may be traced historically. This has led some persons to conclude that since spiritual development may be shown to be continuous, there are no true grounds on which to base the claim of uniqueness for the Christian religion. There need be, however, no contradiction between unbroken historic continuity in the development of man's religious life and a marked departure or unique event occurring at one or more points in the evolutionary process.

Consider, for example, the biological developments which have been traced, stage by stage, from amoeba to man. There is a direct line of evolution from the simplest cellular structure in the animal kingdom to man's complex physical body. The evolution of form from the one kingdom to the other is continuous and unbroken. Yet it cannot be said that the animal is a lower stage of human development or, conversely, that man is only a more highly developed animal. There is what Swedenborg called a discrete degree differentiating the one kingdom from the other.

One may ask then, what is it that determines this line of demarcation between the two kingdoms? What is it that places forms belonging to a single unbroken line of development into either the animal or human categories? We answer, it is the introduction of an added factor into the physical organism at a certain point in its development. Another principle in nature becomes operative. Thus, when the animal organism reaches the stage where the germinal faculty of mind can be incorporated into its structure with the result of making individualization possible, a new kingdom comes into being. Man (*manas*, mind) appears on the scene. Henceforth the individualized virgin spark, the ego which up to this point functioned outside its developing vehicle, becomes indwelling. The "I" or "I AM" is born.

Something similar took place in the unfolding spiritual life of humanity. When the Cosmic Ego, the Christ Principle, actually incarnated in humanity, it commenced to work with that "which we call the race of men" not, as hitherto, from without, but from within the very soul of the collective entity. This is what happened at the time of the Divine Incarnation.

Christianity is indeed the product of all religious experience preceding it. In the words of Manly Hall, "The religious instinct in man is certainly unhistorical, but the unfoldment of that instinct constitutes a valid historical record." The spiritual aspirations that took form in the great pre-Christian religions were foundational to their still ampler expression in Christianity. The religion of Christ was a flowering from out of the past which, in turn, provided a seed for the future. Through the Divine Incarnation a redemptive impulse was released into the human racial stream in an unprecedented manner. It was a special cosmic act neither contradicting nor interfering with the normal and natural evolutionary process, but supporting it. It was a divine enactment done once, once only, and for all time. By virture of this sublime deed, possibilities are present for men to work out their own salvation and attain their destined goal. This event, this entry of the Christ power into the very organic structure of the human race and onto the plane of history, gives to Christianity its distinctive claim to uniqueness among the religions of the world.

From what has just been said it must not be concluded that the race has finished with teachings given by earlier religions. Far from it. The eminent occultist, Rudolf Steiner, makes the statement that many, many centuries will pass before mankind will measure up to the lofty moral concepts enunciated by the Buddha, and yet more ages before humanity attains what may be spoken of as the Christed life. The former will be attained when the race comes into a true understanding of the nature of love; the later stage, when it will not only understand love's nature but will be capable of its actual manifestation. Christ did not merely give teachings *about* love; He became its very incarnation. Hence, not for ages to come will man be able to live Christianity in its fullness.

Thus there are two facts that should be held in mind in connection with Christianity: first, that it is a product and extension of man's past religious experience; second, that with its advent a new divine impulse became active within the composite life of mankind. The two facts are not mutually exclusive. The one accords with the natural law of evolution; the other with the introduction of an added evolutionary factor. In Christianity that added factor was imparted by the Christ. It was an action made necessary by an earlier introduction into the life of humanity of an inimical influence not belonging to its natural evolution, namely, the activity of an interloping host of spirits whom we know as the Lucifers. Christ's incarnation counteracted that which the Lucifers had injected into human life. It is the story of the Fall as related in Genesis, and of Redemption as recounted in the Gospels. Paul summed it up in the words, "For as in Adam all die, so in Christ, shall all be made alive." The false light of Lucifer, the fallen angel, was overcome by the true light of the archangelic Christ.

Such are the cosmic occurrences in relation to human evolution as expounded in works on esoteric Christianity—as, for example, Max Heindel's *Rosicrucian Cosmo-Conception* which sets forth on spiritually scientific grounds the uniqueness of Christianity among the various great religions and divine revelations.

The Dead Sea Scrolls reveal the existence among the Essenes of concepts, beliefs, practices and writings that in many instances anticipated those of the early Christians, so fear has been voiced lest they undermine or actually destroy the convictions long held by Christians that the content of their religion originated with the coming of Christ; that theirs is the only true religion, and that it along has in it the power of salvation. There would be no occasion for such fears if the claim of Christianity's uniqueness were not divorced from its historical background and development. Contrariwise, students of comparative religion would have no difficulty in finding a logical basis for the peculiar distinction claimed by Christianity if, in addition to their historical research, they also investigated what spiritual science reveals.

The esotericist, therefore, is confronted with a double task: To the student of comparative religion the fact to be stressed is Christianity's uniqueness; to the sectarian-minded Christian the fact to be emphasized is the historical development of the universal spirit of the Christos in the life of mankind, culminating in Christ's earthly incarnation. The historical research of the former and the belief in a mystical fact by the latter must not be disturbed or destroyed. There is room for both the historical and the mystical aspects. Not only is there room for both, but each is necessary to the other if we are to grasp the true nature and full significance of a religion which, with its advent, divided time into *before* and *after*

A short-sighted study of comparative religion resting solely on historical grounds may incline one toward indifference to, or rejection of, all religions. On the other hand, narrow insistence on Christianity's uniqueness tends toward religious bigotry. It sets up a barrier that divides instead of revealing principles that unite. The Christos belongs to all peoples and all religions. Before Him every knee shall bow and every tongue confess His holy name. Before this can be, inclusiveness, not exclusiveness, must become the keyword of Christian evangelizers. Buddha, Confucius, Hermes, Zoroaster and other founders of great religions are not to be renounced. The Christ comes to the followers of all religions, not to deprive them of their several faiths, but to let His face shine upon them and to further illumine and empower them in their aspirations for universal Light, the Light of the World.

The Dead Sea Scrolls contain material that should prove helpful in rounding out the prevailing views of both comparative religionists and orthodox Christians. Among the pre-Christian Essenes we find much of Christianity already in evidence, thus indicating an imperceptible transition from B.C. into A.D. But we also learn that the Essenes were primarily concerned with preparations for the fulfillment of age-long prophecies concerning the coming of the Messiah, an event unique in all nature and hence inaugurating a new phase in the spiritual development of the race.

It must be remembered that the final stages of the preparation

23

for Christ's advent called for more than a state of expectancy on the part of believers in the approaching fulfillment of messianic prophecies. It was not enough that they be prepared to recognize Him at His coming. Much more was required. Practical steps had to be taken, specific means provided, and a suitable way of life established, all of which would stand ready for the Master's use when He actually embarked upon His day-to-day service to the children of earth. The Essenes did all this. They were suitably organized; they had spiritual understanding and dedication; they cultivated social and religious patterns wherein precepts of the Christ Dispensation, as uttered in the Sermon on the Mount, would fall naturally into place. It was this preparation that enabled the Christ to securely anchor His redemptive spirit into the very life stream of humanity and so insure its retention and progressive influence within our planetary sphere until the Kingdom of the Father, which He came to restore, would once again be established on earth. We quote the words of the British scholar, Prof. John Allegro of the University of Manchester and one of eight members of the staff now editing the scrolls, "What is clear is that there was a well-defined pattern into which Jesus of Nazareth fits." Thus we can see that the manner of life led by Christ Jesus and His Disciples had been introduced into Judea and the wider Palestinean community before their actual arrival.

The Essenes and the Early Christians

Parallels between the Essenian forerunners of the Christ and His immediate followers are so many and so intimate as to leave no doubt about their being animated by the self-same spirit, and that spiritual impulses giving life and light to the pre-Christian community were identical with those which flowed into the apostolic church when it took form after Christ's ascension. Both fellowships sounded the same keynote and moved close to the same rhythm, namely, that of the new Christ Dispensation.

In speaking of parallels between the Essene Brotherhood and the primitive Christian communities, Dr Cross, in his artiles in *The Christian Century* previously referred to, observes that a close

24

likeness is "to be found in their theological language, in their theology of history, in their liturgical institutions and their ecclesiastical organizations. They apply similar terms to themselves; they are the people of the New Testament who have chosen the Way (cf. Acts 9:2, etc.). Love of God and neighbor is the sum of the law. They are the poor in the world, the children of light, the elect of God who shall judge Israel and the nations at the end of days (I Cor. 6:2-3). They have been given an inheritance in the lot of the holy ones (Col. I12). It is in these areas," concludes Dr. Cross, "that the Essene documents are radically important for our understanding of Christian origins and for the exegesis and definition of New Testament expressions and concepts."

In the discovery of *The Dead Sea Scrolls* the world comes into possession of new documentation dealing with the central point in human history: the coming to the earth of the Lord Christ. To our age it is like a new revelation. To again quote Dr. Cross, the discovery is "bringing undreamed of new illumination to the study of Biblical literature and unhoped for new sources for an understanding of the conceptual world in which Christianity found its historical origin. For careerists in these fields this is exciting enough. For religious scholars it is as though God had added to His 'once for all revelation.' "

To the above we would venture to add that from an esoteric point of view the most arresting feature in connection with the recovered scrolls may well be the added documentary evidence it places in the hands of the general public corroborating esoteric teachings about the Essenes who literally cradled the Christ Child and the Christian faith.

Students of the Christian Mysteries have always known that Joseph and Mary, parents of Jesus, were associated with the Community of the New Covenant; also Elizabeth and Zachariah, parents of John the Batist; and that both John the Forerunner and Jesus the Nazarine grew up under the influence of "The Elect"—as the Essenes regarded themselves by virtue of what they really knew to be their divine historic assignment.

Joachim and Hanna, parents of Mary, were also Initiates of the Essenian Mysteries, a fact made evident by ancient narratives

25

recounting their manner of life. "Saint Paul," says Professor Allegro, "is seen to stand at many points in a direct line of tradition with the Qumran sectarians." Another commentator has suggested that St. Paul contacted the Essenes at Damascus during his three-year sojourn in Syria after his conversion, as recorded in his Epistle to the Galatians, while Mme. Blavatsky makes the positive statement that Paul was an Initiate of the Essene Order. These facts, hitherto but little known, are now in the open. They are salutary, liberalizing truths on the way to becoming common knowledge.

Timed Events

Important events of this kind do not fall out haphazardly. They come to pass when the time is ripe for their emergence. They are called forth by man's thoughts, by the inner activity of his spirit, by his soul's needs. The discovery of *The Dead Sea Scrolls* is clearly such a timed event. The present religious revival and spiritual renewal that is everywhere manifest has created such a state of mind that earnest seekers after deeper truths can profit in a tremendously important way from what the scrolls reveal. It is safe to say that never in the course of the two thousand years during which they have remained hidden could their uncovering have had the significance that it has at this particular time. The questions they answer have not yet been asked so generally nor with such insistence. Today the contents of the scrolls, together with their many implications, are of first importance. Such is the tension, the inner and outer stress and strain of these terribly confused, chaotic and tragic times, that any evidence touching upon the validity of the spiritual basis whereon the Christian faith rests, is eagerly grasped by the many striving to pass from skepticism to faith. The right mood is present, an honest approach is here, and the need for strengthening foundations of faith was never so urgent. So the scrolls have come to light at just the right psychological time. Were it not for these esoteric factors, ever operative in our individual and collective lives, these priceless manuscripts would most certainly continue to slumber in the unknown dark.

From the viewpoint of practical consideration one may well ask how these documents escaped discovery until this late date, when archeological explorations have been going on intensely in every portion of the Holy Land for long periods past and with special thoroughness during the last few decades. Moreover, there were strong leads to the present finds that, it would seem, searching archeologists could scarcely have missed. For example, the Essenes were an established organization. Secular history verifies this fact. They occupied a known area which Pliny located with exactness. In that area ancient ruins have always been known, yet never before completely investigated. Also, it might reasonably be suspected that when Roman legions overran the country at a period coinciding with the disappearance from history of the Essene community, keepers of the latter's treasures might well have sought to preserve them from destruction by concealing them in nearby caves. This is exactly what they did. Yet it remained for an apparently accidental entry by a Bedouin shepherd to set into motion a systematic exploration of the whole surrounding area, with the result that the world has now come into possession of the most remarkable and significant documentary discovery of all times. Although we appear to have come upon them by chance, the discovery occurs under a timing process beyond our ability to trace in its particulars, though we can recognize it in principle. Subtle forces at work under the surface of things and events take shape in obedience to laws operating below, as well as above, the level of conscious human planning.

Multiple Discoveries

An intensely interesting item tending to corroborate the foregoing observation relative to the proper timing for an event to come to pass was reported in the *New York Times*, August 13, 1956. Under a London date line the dispatch reports the discovery of scrolls near the Dead Sea in July 1878, over three-quarters of a century ago. Like the first find of the present discoveries, it was made by Arabs in a cave hewn from rock facing the Dead Sea, though on the shore opposite the recent find. An antique dealer in Jerusalem, Mr. Shapiro by name, acquired these scrolls and in 1883 offered them to the British Museum for a million pounds. Exerts were called in to pass on their genuineness and pronounced them a forgery, shortly after which Mr. Shapiro, humiliated and distraught, committed suicide. Now the dispute is revived. Professor Menshem Mansoor of the Hebrew Department of the University of Wisconsin, in gathering information from many quarters of Europe relative to the recently discovered scrolls, chanced to learn about the manuscripts found years ago. Up to the writing of this reort the British Museum had not been able to exhume the records; but from their translation and other data contained in the Shapiro dossier, Professor Mansoor believes them to be genuine manuscripts belonging to the same period and the same people as the scrolls of recent discovery. The Shapiro manuscripts had the misfortune of coming to light nearly a century too soon, only to be buried again in the basement caverns of the British Museum.

Another related item appeared in the *Los Angeles Times* under a Cairo date line on Oct. 26, 1956. It tells of documents found near Luxor in 1945 and reported as being "one of the greatest archeological finds in history, comparable to the Dead Sea Scrolls." The papyrus manuscripts date from 200 A. D. There are forty-eight "books," the most important of which is entitled *This is the Gospel of Thomas Containing Sayings of Jesus*. Scholars working on the documents have identified this Thomas as one of the Immortal Twelve.

This discovery came very nearly meeting the same fate as did the scrolls found in 1878. The treasures were uncovered by Egyptian workmen who had no idea of their worth. Nor did the businessman who chanced to acquire them suspect their value. It was only after a winding trail that led into Europe and back into the land of their origin that they finally came to repose in the Coptic Museum in Cairo, where experts are at present struggling to decipher and interpret their content. It was by government seizure that Egypt came into possession of its own.

The Dead Sea Scrolls have served to bring into fresh light two other hitherto obscure manuscripts originally found in an old synagogue in Cairo in 1896 and given publication in 1910 under the title *Fragments of a Zadokite Work*. Pieced together, these writings are now usually referred to as the *Damascus Document..*

These manuscripts take on greater meaning because of information acquired from *The Dead Sea Scrolls*. They leave no doubt that the Zadokites who authored them were Essenes belonging to the company of forerunners whose center was in the Judean desert. Prior to the discovery of *The Dead Sea Scrolls* this relation was not certain. Five decades had to pass before they emerged into the clear light in which we now see them.

The close connection that apparently existed between the Damascus and Dead Sea communities has led to conjectures that the Essenes residing in the Dead Sea settlement may have transferred their main activities to Damascus when the Romans under Pompey captured Jerusalem in 63 B.C., an event marking the beginning of the Roman period in Palestine. If so, dated Roman coins and other things found in the caves indicate that they returned to reoccupy for another period their temporarily forsaken quarters. However that may be, there seems to be no doubt that with the collapse of the Jewish revolt in 66-68 A.D., the community was scattered and their monastery, school and library were destroyed by Roman legions. Then, if not on a previous withdrawal, the desert company surely made every effort to preserve their precious library by concealing it in hope of later discovery by those who would recognize its value and profit thereby. To make the preservation of their writings doubly and trebly sure, many of the manuscripts were wrapped in linen, then covered with pitch, and finally placed in sealed earthen jars. Incidently, radio carbon tests applied to the wrappings of linen, an organic substance, have given final corroboration to the approximate dates when the manuscripts were stored away for safety. Such tests are based on measuring the rate of carbon disintegration of a piece of organic material. So the Essenes really managed to preserve for posterity something of their invaluable library and also to leave various "signatures" relative to the period in which they functioned as an organized body, and certain circumstances and events attending their activities.

One more item serves to emphasize how streamers of light of the new day are falling on the Ancient Wisdom. It is recorded in Professor Dupont-Sommer's work, previously referred to, and deals with an Oriental discovery which has for the East a value comparable to that of the Judean discovery for the West. Probably under circumstances of military invasion like those of the Romans into Palestine, a monastery library in Chinese Turkestan was placed in a cave for safety. After a lapse of nine centuries a Tibetan monk "accidentally"came upon the hidden treasure. By 1908 twenty thousand uncovered scrolls were being worked upon, resulting in "a greatly enriched knowledge of the language and history of the Far East."

The Divine Gnosis Is One

The Divine Gnosis has always existed. Christ came to establish conditions under which that Gnosis became more readily accessible. Doors to Initiation, previously closed to all but a few who could undergo severe requirements and under abnormal conditions, were thrown open to whosoever will by the deed of Christ. What had hitherto taken place in the secrecy of Temples of Initiation was enacted openly on the plane of history.

Gnosis is the Greek word for knowledge. Divine Gnosis is knowledge that has become wisdom, the wisdom of Initiates. This wisdom has never been absent from the world. Age after age it has been transmitted to those qualified to receive it. It was in possession of the Essene community that prepared for the Planetary Initiator, the Christ, and those immortal Disciples who came immediately after.

The Divine Gnosis they all held in common recognized initiatory truths that had found manifold expressions in other religions, cultures and civilizations. Among the Essenes one evidence of this has been previously alluded to: the similiarity at many important points in their doctrines and practices with those of Persian Zoroastrians to their east and of Grecian Pythogoreans to their west.

That these same universal elements of man's historical religious development were also present among early Christians has just come to light in literally colorful discovery of an old catacomb in Rome by Vatican archeologists. According to a *Los Angeles Times* dispatch from Rome, April 15, 1956, the priest in charge is quoted as saying, "Nothing like this has ever been found in an early Christian cemetery." The difference? It contained frescoes of mythological as well as bibical subjects! Besides Old Testament scenes depicting Eden, the Flood, Noah, Lot and Wife, the sacrifice of Isaac, Moses in the Bullrushes, Samson Throwing the Lion, and so on, and scenes from the New Testament portraying Jesus with His Disciples, Jesus with Peter and Paul, Jesus and the Samaritan Woman, the Annunciation, Sermon on the Mount, the Raising of Lazarus, and yet other persons and events—in addition to these there were frescoes illustrating pagan myths.

Now the Bible of the Grecians, which took a mythological form, was spiritually apprehended. It was composed of pictorial transcriptions of clairvoyant observations of activities on inner planes of nature as these were related to human and earthly evolution. This the early Christians recognized. So some of these myths were reproduced in the catacombs and preserved, along with corresponding truths that had found literary expression in Hebrew Scriptures and, later, in unfolding Christian revelations.

This inner relationship between the world's great religions, recognized by spiritually enlightened leaders of the times with which we are dealing, were lost sight of in later days when the priesthood ceased to be recruited through Initiation. Hence the discovery of pagan myths represented alongside Biblical scenes comes as a mystifying surprise. A report on the discovery made by the Pontifical Commission of Sacred Archeology states that the "archeologists were amazed that such subjects were chosen to embellish the tombs of early Christians."

These mythological frescoes portrayed, among other figures, Demeter, the Goddess of Abundance. To the Greeks this goddess represented the fruitfulness of the living body of the earth.

The Demeter Mysteries have a Christian analogy. Persephone, daughter of Demeter, is carried away by Pluto to the underworld where her mother after a search discovers her installed as a queen. "This myth," observes Mme Blavatsky, "was transcribed by the Church into the legend of St. Anna going in quest of her daughter Mary, who has been conveyed by Joseph into Egypt."

Then there is an entire cubicle dedicated to the Twelve Labors of Hercules. What are these but a picturization of the twelve facets of character to be developed under the celestial tutelage of the twelve zodiacal Hierarchies? This Greek myth has its Biblical parallel in the twelve labors of Samson as related in the Book of Judges. Incidently Samson, like John the Baptist, was a Nazarite, or Essene, before the latter came into use. Also like John the Baptist, he was a forerunner of the Christ, having been consecrated to God before his birth as one who should, according to a passage in Judges, "begin to save Israel out of the hands of the Philistines"—Philistines representing Biblically the Adversary. Like the Essenes, the Nazarites vowed total abstinence from all intoxicating liquors and complete consecration to God.

Again, the myth of Hercules parallels the life of Samson in that they both relate to the Sun's annual passage through the Zodiac and the labors that man has to accomplish under the successive radiations of each of the twelve zodiacal Hierarchies. Hercules was looked upon as a symbol of the Sun, as was Samson, whose name literally means sunlight or "a little sun." Truly, the Christians had ample reason to include the myth of Hercules in sacred chambers of their hidden catacombs. There would have been no amazement on the part of present-day discoverers over finding such conceptions portrayed by the early Christians had not the Wisdom Teachings, possessed alike by the Essenes and their immediate successors, been quite neglected, then almost forgotten and finally completely rejected by Christian orthodoxy. As Albert Pike observes, "even those who embraced Christianity mingled together the old and the new, Christianity and philosophy, the apostolic teachings and the traditions of mythology... Accordingly, the distinction between the esoteric and the exoteric doctrine....easily gained a foothold among many of the Christians... The writings of the Essenes were full of mysticism, parables, enigmas and allegories. They believed in the esoteric and exoteric meanings of

32

the scriptures... They found it in the Old Testament as the Gnostics found it in the New." These inner and outer meanings are affirmed by the Christ when telling His Disciples that it was given to them to know the mysteries of the Kingdom of God, but to those who are without it was not given. And Paul, in referring to this same distinction, speaks of giving milk to babes but meat to the strong.

So we find that the recent portrayals discovered in a Christian catacomb provide added archeological corroboration for modern man's contemplation of the Gnostic thesis that the early Christians, both before and after Christ's advent, recognized correlative values in other and earlier religious systems, the deepest meaning of which lay hidden underneath the written word or pictorial representation. Christian mysticism develops this aspect of spiritual philosophy to considerable lengths. It asserts that Christianity, while unique and bearing within it a divine impulse of a strength and quality not previously present in the world, will nevertheless fail to be rightly or fully understood without reference to its age-long background and the progressive development of human consciousness, with a growing capacity for receiving, absorbing and manifesting ever more of universal Light, Love and Life.

PART TWO

THE SCROLLS SEVERALLY CONSIDERED

Commentary on the Book of Habakkuk

 he *Habakkuk Commentary* is an Essenian work never before known. Aside from the philological interest of recovering a more ancient text, even as in the case of the *Isaiah Scroll*, its chief interest lies in the light it throws on religious thought in the intratestamental period and, more particularly, the information it contains about the specific forerunners of the Christ, the Essenes.

Only the first two of the Book's three chapters are covered by the *Commentary*. This fact tends to substantiate Biblical critics who believe the third chapter was a later addition and may not even have been written when the *Commentary* was prepared.

The *Book of Habakkuk* dates from about the sixth century B.C. Its message of a redeemed earth and a regenerated humanity is considered one of the most inspired of all Old Testament passages. Very appropriately did it become the subject for Essenian exposition, dedicated as this group was to preparing the world to receive the Redeemer.

The interpretation is not concerned with the historical aspects of the Book of Habakkuk. It is primarily allegorical. It is the inner mystical content of the Book that is the chief concern of the commentator. The Mystery Wisdom is in the background of the readings. "It is with the help of symbols they expound their philosophy," writes Philo.

The *Commentary* does make allusions throughout to unnamed contemporary characters and events to be found in historical records of the time. Most important of these references are those relating to the founder of the Essene Brotherhood, to which the commentator presumably belonged. This personage is referred to by various descriptive titles, such as the Teacher of Righteousness, the Master of Justice and other similar terms. It is stated that he was a priest who received divine revelations, who could interpret the law and the prophets, and who was commissioned by God to communicate his revelations to his people; that he founded a community called The New Covenant and gathered about him disciples who were placed under strict disciplines. Further, that since he carried on his ministry apart from the established religious organization, he incurred the hostility of the priesthood at Jerusalem until it finally had him condemned and put to death.

The Isaiah Scroll

The Isaiah manuscript, which dates from about 100 B.C., is virtually complete and in the form as we know it. The discovered text shows a number of variants from the accepted version but none are regarded by Bible scholars as of great importance. It has, however, been responsible for a few changes in the reading of the *Revised Standard Version*. But what Biblical scholars have most valued in the *Isaiah Scroll* is the archaic Hebrew text for a large part of the Bible, a text several centuries earlier than the accepted Masoretic (rabbinical) text of the eighth century A.D. The oldest examples of the latter are of the ninth or tenth century, while the Dead Sea manuscripts are about a thousand years older.

Professor Dupont-Sommer thinks it is no mere accident that the two *Isaiah Scrolls* were found, and in so perfect a condition. "Indeed," says he, "the book of Isaiah—the first and most important of the prophetic writings of the Old Testament—is the one which pious Jews liked most of all to read and to meditate on in the centuries to which we assign the discoveries." He then recalls Luke's account of how Jesus, entering a synagogue in Nazareth and standing up to read, was handed the Book of Isaiah.

And "unrolling the book he found the passage where it is written: The spirit of the Lord is upon me... Then he rolled up the book and returned it to the attendants and sat down." And then there was the minister of the Queen of Ethiopia, mentioned in the Acts of the Apostles, who was sitting in his chariot reading the Book of Isaiah, and, significantly, it was about the coming Messiah. It is a fanciful thought, yet not too remote from the possible, that the *Isaiah Scroll* unrolled today was circulating when the above incidents occurred and could be the very copy from which the Master read or from which the studious Ethiopian sought spiritual light and comfort.

The second *Isaiah Scroll* contains the last third of the Book of Isaiah, which Biblical scholars call the *Deutero-Isaiah*, or Second Isaiah, because it was apparently written by a different author than the first part. It tells of a gentle, humble, suffering servant who will come to redeem humanity.

Psalms of Thanksgiving

Under this designation are thirty-five psalms hitherto completely unknown. They are thought to have been composed by the Essene Initiate Leader, the Teacher of Righteousness himself, or written in honor of him by a disciple who served as the Prophet's messenger. They radiate glorious faith, deep spirituality and a glowing sense of the protecting and directing power of a Divine Presence. In form they are patterned after the Psalms of the Old Testament; in spirit they belong to the New. This is perhaps the most remarkable feature of the *Psalms of Thanksgiving*, as some commentators have observed. They blend a past inheritance and an emerging future. In one of their psalms, according to Professor Allegro, the people of these hymns picture themselves as a woman in the pangs of childbirth bringing forth a new order of things. In the words of Dupont-Sommer, "If the spiritual songs of the New Covenant keep the expressions of the Old Covenant, the general sense and spirit are different. In actual fact, it is new wine which has been poured into old bottles."

There is a lyric beauty in the composition of the hymns and

37

they are fragrant with a deep spirituality and a joy that could come only from the serene depths of souls firmly anchored in the eternal. They convey such a sense of unity with the divine that even in the midst of trial and tragedy, they sing exultantly of secure centeredness in that which is unshakable and ever-abiding. "Thou hast illumed my face by Thy covenant... Then, like a veritable dawn, like Destiny, Thou didst appear unto me." Such is the lofty tone running through the *Psalms of Thanksgiving*.

War of the Sons of Light Against the Sons of Darkness

The document so titled is a blend of history and mysticism. The historical background is the struggle between the Israelites and the native tribes of Palestine. The combatants on both sides are mentioned by name. Organization of the military forces is set forth in precise detail. The army is divided into thousands, hundreds, fifties and tens. It is made up in four classes. The manner of their maneuvering is carefully described and so, too, that of accompanying noncombatant priests. The ritual of battle indicates the same emphasis on trumpets and horns as it does on the hurling of sling-shots and javelins. Sound and number are employed with seemingly scientific knowledge of their magical properties. The numbers three, four and ten enter into the army formation; the number seven, into action. Seven times the stones must be thrown and seven times the javelins are to be hurled. The trumpets are to signal readiness for battle and launching of the attack; they are to sustain the army during the battle and to signal its victory with appropriate notes of triumph.

The spiritual aspect of this battle is emphasized by mottoes affixed to army insignia. One set is used when going into battle; another set while engaged in combat; yet another on returning from the strife. And in every instance the appeal, the affirmation or the praise and thanksgiving, as the case may be, is to God.

This document is obviously not intended to serve primarily as a military manual or historical record, though it may be basically true to the physical organization and external events which it sets forth. It tells of a cosmic war between God and Belial, the Prince

38

of Darkness. It is a stepped-down version of the war in heaven between Michael and his angels and Lucifer with all his hosts. Incidentally, the last of the *Thanksgiving Hymns* is addressed to Michael, he whose countenance is like that of the Sun and who ranks in the solar Hierarchy next to Christ.

Also, the document is another version, adapted to Essenian times and environment, of the Zoroastrian account of the battle between Ormuzd, the God of Light, and Ahriman, the Power of Darkness. John the Evangelist opens his Gospel on this very theme. The Word that was in the beginning was the "light of men," the "true light"which shone in darkness but the darkness comprehended it not. In the scroll version this power of darkness sought to extinguish the light, but without success; in the end, light prevailed. Hence the conflict and tragedy, with ultimate victory for truth, for good, for light. Such is the outcome traced in both the Essene War of the Sons of Light and in the Gospel according to St. John. Both versions were the product of the same age, the same people, the same quality of life, the same type of illumined consciousness. Both have to do primarily with the battle waged by the opposites within man's own nature and not with any external conflict. As voiced by Goethe:

> Two souls, alas, are housed within my breast, And struggle
>   And struggle there for undivided reign;
> And one to the earth with passionate desire
>   And closely clinging organs still adheres,
> Above the mists the other does aspire
>   With sacred ardor unto purer spheres.

The sole purpose of the Essene way of life was to effect purification and regeneration of the imperfect human personality to make it a fit temple for the living God.

One section of the *Manual of Discipline*, with which we shall deal more fully presently, treats with man's dual nature, one coming under the spirit of truth and the other under the spirit of perversion. It is the "prince of light"struggling with the "angel of darkness." Mankind is said to be divided in allegiance to these two opposing powers and the inheritance of each is according to the

39

power served. The reading at this point virtually parallels a passage addressed by St. Paul to the Romans, "Know ye not, that to whom ye yield yourselves servants to obey, his servants ye are to whom ye obey; whether of sin unto death, or of obedience unto righteousness."

Similarities between the language of the *Manual* and of Saint Paul occur in so many instances they give one the impression again and again that this is no mere coincidence but is due to a nearness in thought and spirit which existed among the immediate forerunners and the early followers of Christ's earthly ministry.

According to the *Manual* the conflict between the Forces of Light and the Powers of Darkness enabled man to know of good and evil, and that according to God's mysteries the opposing contestants had been "set in equal parts."But this was to be for a time only. Ultimately light would conquer darkness and clear the way for "the making of the New."

It was the task of hastening the process of creating the New—the New Man, the New Dispensation—that the people of the New Covenant set for themselves. They were working toward the day when the Anointed One would come to earth and release a divine impulse that would give humanity the uplift it needed in order to "put off the old man with his deeds, and to put on the new," to again quote Saint Paul.

The Testaments of the Twelve Patriarchs

This is the Essene apocryphal book of which only fragments have been recovered in the recent finds. It is an Aramaic version of several chapters of Genesis, interwoven with stories and legends about the lives of the patriarchs. It contains messages supposedly spoken by each of the twelve sons of Jacob at the time of death. The book is described as full of ideas and language similar on the' one hand to the literature of the Essenes and on the other to that of Christianity. One of the scholars, Dr. R.H. Charles, editing the scroll found seventy words common to the *Testaments* and the Pauline Epistles but not found in the rest of the New Testament. It deals with the Messiah, His redemptive role and the plan of salvation.

As further evidence of the close relationship existing between the Essenes who lived and wrought just before Christ's coming and those who spread His Gospel immediately after His ministry is this assage from the *Testaments* which parallels so closely one in the St. Matthew's Gospel. The Essene version reads:

> I was sold into slavery, and the Lord of all made me free;
> I was taken into captivity, and His strong hand succoured me.
> I was beset with hunger, and the Lord Himself nourished me.
> I was alone, and God comforted me;
> I was sick, and the Lord visited me;
> I was in prison, and my Lord showed favor to me;
> In bonds, and he released me . . .

And this in Matthew:

> For I was hungry and you gave me food,
> I was thirsty and you gave me drink.
> I was a stranger and you welcomed me,
> I was naked and you clothed me,
> I was sick and you visited me,
> I was in prison, and you came to me . . .

Scholars have called attention to other striking similarities in both wording and spirit. The following passage, for example, reads like an utterance by Jesus, "And they who have died in grief shall arise in joy; and they who were poor for the Lord's sake shall be made rich; and they who are put to death for the Lord's sake shall awake to life."

Eusebius of Palestine, sometimes called "The Father of Church History," writing about three centuries after the rise of Christianity, found literature of the Essenes and the related Therapeutae so similar that he regarded them virtually as one. Such testimony is drawn on in support of the thesis that Gospel records are true only as restatements of the Ageless Wisdom of the Mysteries as this pertains to steps and events leading to Illumination, and not as history.

This is last in the list of the seven principal scrolls discovered in recent finds. Like the *Testaments*, it is an Aramaic version of several chapters of Genesis. Lamech is mentioned in Genesis as the son of Methuselah and the father of Noah. Melchizedek, who also comes in for mention in this scroll, is described, even as in Genesis, as King of Salem, the city of peace. The general supposition has been that Salem is none other than Jerusalem. The scroll verifies this interpretation for therein we have the fact appended in the phrase, "Salem, which is Jerusalem." The document tells of Abraham's visit to Egypt, the taking of his wife Sarah, Lot's departure from Sodom and the War of the Five Kings.

Other Old Testament Apocrypha

Fragments of several other Old Testament apocryphal writings have been found scattered throughout many caves, indicating them to have been a part of the Essene library. Scholars think they may have been produced by members of the brotherhood. They also venture the opinion that some, if not all, of these apocryphal writings would have been incorporated in the Hebrew canon had they appeared prior to the date when the Old Testament Scriptures had been finally fixed upon.

Among the apocryphal collection is the *Book of Jubilees*, sometimes called the "Little Genesis." It contains references that have been interpreted as referring to a Messiah from the tribe of Levi.

Another apocryphal work is the *Book of Enoch*, described as having a marked affinity with Gnosticism, Zoroastrianism and Jewish apocalyptic thought. There are references in it to times and seasons, subjects of utmost importance to the Essenes who sought to cultivate a greater awareness of their relationship with the cosmos and who believed there was a right time for every enterprise, a time "desired by God" and "fixed by destiny," an auspicious moment "inscribed in the stars." Josephus reports that they believed "nothing befalls a man but what is according to its

(Fate's) determination," Fate meaning to them the exact operation of divine law and not a negation of free will. This subject is also introduced in the *Book of Jubilees*.

The *Assumption of Moses* is one more of the same group of writings.

We now turn to another scroll of major importance, the *Manual of Discipline* which, for our present study, together with the *Habakkuk Commentary*, is of greatest interest.

Manual of Discipline

This scroll has been also called the *Rule of the New Covenant*. It sets forth something of the organization, practices and beliefs of the Essene community. It expresses sentiments and ideals to be cultivated by members and lays down rules and regulations pertaining to requirements for membership, admission to same, liturgical services, initiatory rites, legal matters, social relationship, disciplinary measures and a specified code of conduct binding upon every individual belonging to the community.

The *Manual* stresses throughout the principle of unity, brotherhood and cooperation. *Community* appears as the keyword of the society—community of property, interests, aspiration, purpose and service. The brothers were a closely-knit band of pioneers who sustained each other against indifference by the many and active opposition and persecution by leaders of both the religious and political orthodoxies of their time. They also recognized that as scattered individuals they could not accomplish what was possible of achievement by joining forces and working unitedly, with singleness of mind and heart, on the big task they had set out to accomplish.

Thus, the members of this esoteric group surrendered their lives completely to the service of God and man. They supported each other in a common quest for truth and in the cultivation of highest moral values. A regenerated life was their aim, and for its realization they willingly submitted themselves to rigid disciplines. Simplicity and humility were cardinal virtues and the transmutation of lower instincts into spiritual power constituted

43

for them the Great Work.

The *Manual* is not exactly what the title suggests. It is not a *Robert's Rules of Order*. The material is neither so concise nor so well ordered. Moreover, its factual content is interspersed with purely literary insertions. As the *Manual* has not been recovered in its completeness, it does not produce the whole picture of Essene community life in all particulars. But many details not found in the *Manual* are recorded in the *Damascus Document* and other contemporary writings.

Membership

From the recovered portions of the *Manual of Discipline* we learn that an applicant for membership was placed on one year's probation. If his conduct proved worthy, two more years of study and testing followed. Then, if favorably passed upon by the priests and the majority of members, he was admitted to full membership and assigned by the Overseer to a specific place and position among his brethren. From that time on not only his property, time and labor but, in the words of the *Manual* "his counsel shall belong to the Community, also his judgment."

Women participated as associate members. Children were placed under a ten-year period of prescribed study. At the age of twenty they were eligible for membership, admission following upon satisfactorily passing a public examination in required subjects and on giving acceptable evidence of sound moral character.

When receiving new members into the order the priests recounted God's righteousness and the grace He had bestowed upon the children of Israel. Of this grace applicants confessed their unworthiness. The priest continued a recital with what is virtually a transcription of a passage in Deuteronomy, "Behold I set before you this day a blessing and a curse; a blessing if ye obey the commandments of the Lord our God...and a curse if ye will not obey..."

Members "enter into the covenant in God's presence." They pledged themselves "to live in true unity and good humility and loving devotion and righteous purpose each toward his fellow in the holy Council and as members of the eternal assembly." The lesser agreed to obey the greater, a difference in rank based solely on varying degrees of responsibility assumed. They dedicated themselves to "His truth" and pledged allegiance to God's ordinance as these were "given by Moses and all God's servants, the prophets." They promised to observe appropriately certain dates marked off on a sacred calendar of their own, to eat communally, and to carry out all their enterprises as a unit.

Holding All Things in Common

On attaining full membership, but not until then, individuals surrendered without reservation all personal possessions to the common store. In the words of the *Manual*, "All who dedicate themselves to His Truth shall bring all their mind and their strength and their property into the Community of God." From then on they sought nothing of the world's goods for themselves alone. In this manner they not only anticipated Christ's admonition to His followers not to lay up for themselves treasures upon earth, but they obeyed the injunction with strict literalness. Writes Philo, they did not "store up treasures of silver and gold" or "acquire vast sections of earth out of a desire for ample revenue." They regarded contentment of mind as the greatest of riches.

As the Christ taught sharing, saying, "He that has two coats let him impart to him that has none; and he that has meat let him do likewise," so did the Essenes. It was from each according to his ability and to each according to his need. Like the early followers of the Master, as reported in the Acts of the Apostles, "They were of one heart and of one soul: neither said any of them that ought of the things which he possessed was his own; but they had all things in common."

The souls that drew nearest to Christ just before His coming and immediately after His earthly sojourn, namely, the Essene community during the former period and the apostolic fellowship during the latter, functioned at a spiritual level where

45

they were capable of practicing *true* communism. Let no one identify that with the political brand bidding for man's allegiance in the world today. The communism of the Essenes was based on a spiritual foundation; the communism of today is based on material grounds. True communism becomes possible only when those practicing it live in accordance with the soul's direction. Individualization has then reached the point where the natural and spontaneous impulses of the whole being are to give, to share, to love, to serve. It then becomes clear that further progress is possible, not by the aggrandizement of personal powers and possessions, but by an outflowing of spiritualized love and selfless service to others. Communism is then a state of collective activity in which every member acts in full freedom and in harmony with the dictates of an awakened spirit.

Poltical and materialistic communism is of quite another type. Communism enforced by compulsion is contrary to the evolutionary process and a barrier to the unfoldment of man's higher spiritual faculties. If this type of communism were to prevail under the materialistic philosophy which now guides it, the spiritual life of humanity would suffer a progressive decline. The spiritual life requires a state of freedom for its proper development. Freedom is the keyword governing its expression. Under repression and compulsion it stultifies and dies.

The Prophetic Function

Before members were admitted to the Mysteries they were obliged to pass three days and three nights of meditation in a lonely grotto. The only food and drink permitted were fruit, bread and water. Such discipline and others of a similar nature, together with their whole way of life, were designed to sensitize and purify aspirants' bodies and to achieve what William Blake described as cleansing "the doors of perception," so they might see more clearly the divine plan of the ages and rightly perform such part toward its fulfillment as they not only felt but inwardly recognized as having been assigned to them. They were forerunners, light-bringers, prophets. As prophets they

46

considered themselves to be in the line of direct succession to the Hebrew prophets and strove to be worthy of the calling.

To the Essenes the Old Testament was more than history—the aspect most prominent in modern man's mind. It was more than the Book of the Law, which was all it meant to the Sadducees. It was to them, above all else, prophecy. It was a record of an unfolding divine pattern of preparation for the coming of the Messiah. Hence, they devoted themselves to cultivating the type of consciousness that would enable them to tune in to the spiritual requirements of the hour and to proclaim them to their generation. Specifically, they sought added light on mysteries connected with man's "fall" and for tracing its consequences, that they might better understand and make known related mysteries underlying steps to be taken for his redemption.

This they succeeded in doing, and the four Gospels bear witness to the fact. While the Essenes are not mentioned by name in these records, John the Baptist, a member of their company of forerunners according to the testimony of contemporary historians, came preaching and prophesying, "Repent ye; for the kingdom of heaven is at hand." And again, "There comes one mightier than I after me... Indeed I baptize you with water but he shall baptize you with the Holy Spirit."

The continuity of the prophetic function from the time of the old Hebrew prophets to the time of their direct descendants, the Essenes, is made clear by St. Matthew in his statement about John, "This is he that was spoken of by the prophet Esaias, saying, The voice of one crying in the wilderness, Prepare ye the way of the Lord, make his paths straight."

It is also significant in this connection that the Pharisees wanted to know John's ancestral identity. Which of the old prophets did he reincarnate? Was he Elias? John said no, but Jesus, speaking of John—who, in His words, came "neither eating nor drinking—" said John was he whose cocoming "all the prophets and law prophesied" as being a messenger who was to prepare the way. To which the Master added pointedly, "If ye will receive it, this is Elias, which was for to come. He that hath ears to hear, let him hear."

47

Zacharias, father of John and, as previously noted, an Essene, also had this prophetic gift. Luke records Zacharias' vision of the role his son was to perform, saying John was the one spoken of by the "holy prophets" as he who was to "go before the face of the Lord to prepare his ways."

Secular history records various instances of the exactness with which some of the Essene predictions concerning people and events of their own time came to fulfillment. Here is one such prediction as given in an article on *The Mystic Order of the Essenes* by Dr. Enid S. Smith, which appeared in the *Rosicrucian Magazine* of December, 1956. "An Essene, Menahem, once met Herod as a boy going to school, and addressed him as 'King of the Jews,' Herod thought the man who did not know him jested, and told him of his common origin with no chance of becoming king. But Menahem smiled at him and clapped him on the shoulder, saying, 'Thou wilt, nevertheless, be king and wilt begin thy reign happily, for God has found thee worthy of it. Remember the blows that Menahem has given thee as a symbol of a change of thy fortune. For this assurance will be salutary for thee when thou wilt love justice and piety toward God and equity toward thy citizens. However, I know thou wilt not be such a one, for I can perceive it all. Thou wilt obtain an everlasting reputation, but thou wilt forget piety and justice. Thou wilt not be concealed from God, for He will visit thee in His wrath for it, towards the end of thy life.'"

A knowledge of cycles and of the particular task or phase of development to be undertaken within a certain time period enters into one's ability to predict future events and the nature of impending changes. Apropos of this, in *Isis Unveiled* Mme. Blavatsky observes that "both Jesus and St. John the Baptist preached the end of the age; which proves their knowledge of the secret computation of the priests and kabbalists, who with the chiefs of the Essene communities alone had the secret of the duration of cycles. The latter were kabbalists and theurgists; they had their mystic books and predicted future events."

All matters pertaining to the community life of the Essenes were subject to the "divinely guided" majority. Theirs was a democratic society functioning under highly disciplined hierarchical order. Membership carried privileges with responsibility. Attendance at meetings was obligatory. The order of assembling is thus described, "First the priests, then the Levites, and next all the people, by thousands, and hundreds, and fifties, and tens according to . . . the status of his office in God's community." Seating arrangements were also prescribed. The members lived by order as "heaven's first law."

Whatsoever the Essenes did was done as unto the Lord. To them the whole of life was a sacred ritual. Their daily ablutions and communal meals took on symbolic meaning. The former anticipated the baptismal rite and the latter the Holy Communion service of the Christian church. Breaking the bread of brotherhood at a common board was an occasion for remembering that man lives not by bread alone. Holy words were spoken. The eucharistic bread and the juice of the grape were dispersed. At the head of the table a priest presided over their simple but ample repast, which opened and closed with thanksgiving prayers and blessings.

Since the Essenes geared their daily life to the absolutes of truth, love, honesty and purity, they could give no place to taking oaths except those required on entering upon Initiation into the sacred Mysteries. Says Josephus, "Everything spoken by them is stronger than an oath. Swearing is shunned by them." When Christ Jesus included in His Sermon on the Mount the precept not to swear at all, "neither by heaven . . . nor the earth" but "to perform unto the Lord thine oaths," He was merely stating what His enlightened forerunners had long practiced.

This is true at many points. For instance, the *Manual* says, "I will repay no man with evils due; only with good will I pursue a man." Said the Christ, "Love your enemies . . . do good to them that hate you." In the *Manual* we read, "For with God is the judgment of every living thing; and He will reward a man with his due." Christ admonished, "Judge not, that ye be not judged." Many similar parallels could be added. Little wonder, therefore, that an ecclesiastical historian like Eusebius, when reviewing the development of Christianity from a prespective of some three centuries, failed to discover any sharp distinction between the writings, beliefs and practices of the immediate forerunners of the Christ and those who came just after His incarnation. This historian actually asserts that the "canonical Christian Gospels and epistles were the ancient writings of the Essenes or their reproduction in the name of Jesus."

In a certain sense this is true, since all the writings in question were composed in the language of the Mysteries. But admitting this does not render, as some would suppose, New Testament Scriptures spurious forgeries or mere reproductions of earlier compositions. Trusting the spiritual investigations of the Christian occultist, Rudolf Steiner, we can rest assured that while the initiatory Wisdom and the Mystery language are the same in Essene writings as they are in the Gospels and Epistles of the New Testament, the latter were no mere copies of something previously produced. Rather, they were fresh, original creations by other illumined souls who contacted the same inner source of divine inspiration as had their Initiate predecessors.

The Community's Council consisted of three priests and twelve laymen. Association with those "who walk in the way of wickedness" was strictly forbidden. Penalties for violating the accepted code were stated, varying according to the trespass, and a terrible fate was pronounced on those who proved to be "traitors to the truth." When there was occasion to reprove a member it was done in private; then, if need be, in the presence of the assembly. Correction was to be given "in truth, humility and loving devotion."

Among the catalogued offenses subject to penalties were, for example, answering "a fellow with a stiff neck," speaking with quick temper or haughtily, rejecting admonitions of senior members, taking the Honored Name in vain, bearing a grudge against one's fellow, uttering words of folly, "laughing foolishly with audible voice." The latter offense drew thirty days, but he who muffled his guffaws with his hands was given only ten days!

Observing Times and Seasons

There are ordinances stipulating certain exercises to be performed regularly at such stated times as dawn and twilight, the "coming together of seasons," the "circuits of the moon," and "holy days in their ordered sequence." The Essenes observed strictly the seventh day and kept it holy. There is also reference to "the weeks of the years" and "to their weeks to a season of release," referring to the year of Jubilee as defined in Leviticus. These are among the ordinances "in which the wise man is taught to walk." The term "wise man" as here used may well be in the same sense as in Genesis where we read of Pharaoh's calling for all "the magicians of Egypt and all the wise men thereof" to come to his aid and in Matthew's account of the "wise men of the East" who come to worship the child Jesus. In each instance the reference is to Ageless Wisdom. That this is the meaning of the term when used in the *Manual* finds corroboration in a passage from the related Damascus Document, which also mentions sabbaths and festivals and the significance of their proper observance as "hidden things in which all Israel went astray." The four Archangels, Gabriel, Raphael, Soriel (Uriel) and Michael—each governing, in the order named, one of the four quarters of the year beginning with the Winter Solstice—are all mentioned in Essene writings.

Wherever the Ancient Wisdom is present and active, in times past or present, there is recognition of the varying quality of hours, days and seasons. There are special times when the tides serve, when the winds give benefit. The wise take advantage of these times. They work in harmony with nature's rhythms. They are mindful of their cosmic citizenship, their universal relationship. In the words of the *Manual*, the members of the brotherhood were "not to take a single step outside any of the works of God, but to accomplish them in their time: not to anticipate their moments, nor to be late." New Moons, Full Moons, the Solstices and the Equinoxes are such times. The Mystery Schools of ancient days observed these cosmically determined dates with appropriate rites and ceremonials. Their sacred calendar conformed to the ordinances of the heavens. Their observances had celestial authenticity. All this was present as wisdom and practice among the Essenes.

Many particulars contained in the *Manual of Discipline* were known previously through such writers as the three alalready mentioned—Josephus, Pliny and Philo. The recovered scrolls confirm the reliability of their reports and observations. They also provide additional information. Josephus, for instance, states that a probationer on entrance into the society was given white clothing, a loin cloth and a small mattock. These were the external symbols of the order. At the time of Initiation, states the Jewish historian, a new member vowed to keep faith with all men, to be a lover of truth, to expose liars, to keep his hands from theft and his soul free from unholy gain, to conceal nothing from fellow members, to divulge none of the order's deeper secrets to outsiders, and that the code governing the society would be transmitted to successors exactly as it had been received.

Dietary Regimen

A disciplined life is essential to spiritual attainment. The particular disciplines required vary in time and place and at different stages of man's development. With every advancing degree they become more exacting. But with all these variations, certain basic principles are common to all aspirants on the path. The direction for them is to live a harmless life and to adopt the kind of regimen that most effectively contributes to the transmutation of their lower nature into a higher. One practice to this end adopted by the Essenes was not to take life unnecessarily and to nourish their bodies on the pure, passionless products of the plant kingdom. This injunction was practiced by both the Pythagoreans and the Zoroastrians.

Undoubtedly these three Schools influenced each other. In the last analysis, however, all esoteric societies, wherever located and independently of each other, draw their guiding principles from one and the same Hierarchy of Light of which the Universal Christos is the ackowledged head. Each contributes to the others. Each cultivates some special phase of the evolutionary process and of man's ever-developing consciousness.

Note, for example, parallels pertaining to diet and reverence for life among the Essenes, the Pythagoreans and the Zoroastrians. Consider the Essenes first. This religious group looked to the Mosaic law which commanded, "Thou shalt not kill" and to the dietary regimen prescribed for edenic man by the Lord God in the opening or creation chapter of Genesis, "Behold, I have given you every herb-bearing seed which is upon the face of the earth and every tree in which is the fruit of a tree yielding seed; to you it shall be meat." This divine direction they followed.

Julius Selinus, a third century Roman writer, gave it as his opinion that the Essenes had been "appointed by divine Providence for this mode of life." He speaks of their "marvelous constitutions," as does Josephus who said that because of their simplicity of diet and their well-ordered way of living, many members lived to be a hundred years old. They sought to live by the axiom of purification as later given by the Theosophical teacher, Annie Besant, "Pure thoughts, pure food and a constant memory of God." In the words of the *Manual*, they were "to purify their intelligence in the truth of the precepts of God and to regulate their strength according to the perfection of His ways." Also, "To keep from all evil and to cling to all good works; to practice truth, justice and right . . . and not to walk in the stubbornness of a guilty heart, lustful glances, so as to do no evil . . . "

As to animal sacrifices required of the ancient Israelites, while the Essenes as a Jewish sect stressed obedience to the Mosaic law, they moved so far in advance of the Old Dispensation and approached so close to the New that they abandoned animal sacrifice as a mere outer symbol of the sacrifice to be made within themselves of their own animal propensities. "They serve God," says Philo, "not by sacrificing animals, but by seeking to order their thoughts duly in accord with holiness." So firmly did they lay hold of the inner reality that they could afford to dispense with the outer symbol. They sent gifts to the Temple, but the priesthood claimed this did not satisfy the demands of the Mosaic Law, in consequence of which they were excluded from the Temple precincts.

As in diet, so in dress. ⅃he Essenes wore no woolens; their clothing, oike their food, was derived from the plant kingdom. And their garments were white out of respect to the white light of spirit which they aimed to manifest by purity in their lives. According to the *Manual*, they sought "to be united in the Party of God so that they might walk before Him in perfection . . . and so . . . love all the sons of light." Their salutation was "Peace be with you."

Note now the similarity between the foregoing Essenian teaching and practice and that of the Zoroastrians. From the *Oaspe* "Bible" we quote, "So they built altars to Ormuzd, and taught the people worship, and caused them to take an oath not to kill any man or woman or child, nor beast, nor bird; nor any animal created alive. And they bound them on oath to eat only fruit and nuts and roots and bread, according to the Ozmuzdian law. And they divided them into families of tens and families of hundreds and of a thousand, giving them one rab'bah for each, according to the Zoroastrian law."

All this is concurred in by the Pythagoreans, a subject dealt with in its several aspects—hygienic, ethical and spiritual—in *Pythagoron*, a reconstruction by Hobart Huson of the teachings of Pythagoras. "The simplest and most natural foods," asserts this Greek philosopher, "partaken in virginal state, as nearly as possible, are best for man . . . No one can love fellow creatures and shed their blood without stern necessity. Much less eat them . . . Keep the precept of Orpheus . . . And keep thyself from the eating of food which has had life . . . Oh mortals! do not pollute your bodies with food so impious . . . The earth, prodigal of her wealth, supplies you her kindly sustenance and offers you food without bloodshed and slaughter."

Such were the precepts of Moses, Zoroaster and Pythagoras which the Essenes perpetuated in their teachings and in their disciplined, regenerative way of life.

To the foregoing correspondences found in three important ancient esoteric societies and touching upon a particular exercise as an aid toward purification of body and soul, we quote another from a modern exponent of the higher life. It is from Dr. Rudolf Steiner's volume on *The Gospel of St. Matthew*. In speaking of the dietary practices of the Essenes, and also of the Nazarenes whose ways of life were so similar, he states that their abstention "from meat and wine made a certain enlightenment possible, for it is a fact that the consumption of meat can be a hindrance to the path when striving for spiritual development. Without implying any propaganda on behalf of vegetarianism," he goes on to say, "it is a fact that abstention from meat makes everything easier, for in that case the soul increases in strength and in power of endurance, and is stronger to overcome the oppositions and hindrances arising from the physical and etheric bodies. Capacities for endurance increase by abstaining from flesh though it is not such abstinence alone, but all the things connected with it that tend to strengthen the soul."

It is quite fitting that Dr. Steiner should be introduced at this point in association with the Essenes, since he took it as his highest mission to do for this generation exactly what the Essenes did for theirs, namely, to help groping souls find the way to Christ.

One of the most prominent features of the Essenian way of life was their scrupulous attention to Levitical laws of cleanliness. Various forms of ritual ablutions were prescribed. Cleansing of the body was taken as symbolical of an inner cleansing if done invoking, as they did, the waters of life to wash away all worldly stain. When John the Forerunner baptized Jesus in the Jordan the performance was essentially Essenian in character. From that hallowed act, baptism became one of the sacraments of the Christian church. Professor Dupont-Sommer makes out a very plausible case for Essenian participation in

55

preparation for the Master's last supper with the Twelve. This authority says the waterbearer whom the Disciples were bidden to follow was an Essene and that the house to which they all repaired was one where members of the brotherhood were accustomed to hold ceremonial meals and to perform daily ablutions.

Social Organization

The "city of the widlerness" by the Dead Sea was made up of one large structure with several smaller houses adjoining it. These were first thought to be merely remnants of a Roman fort, and they may have been so used after the city's desertion by the Essenes. For long these ruins have remained largely buried under sand and debris but have now come in for extensive excavations with richly rewarding results. The main building is found to contain large communal kitchens, dining halls, wash rooms, large and small cisterns, and a scriptorium where manuscripts were composed and copied.

As previously stated, the Essenes established small centers of activity at various points in Palestine and beyond. The centers were organized along military lines since they recognized a need for close organization, strict discipline, simple living and effective action as warriors of God called to clear the way for the approaching Savior of the World. They had their own councils whereby justice was dispensed with mercy.

There were two leaders at the head of each camp, a priest and an administrator. This was as it is today in Tibet where the Dalai Lama presides over purely spiritual matters and the Panchen Lama over civil matters, but for the latter position spiritual qualifications are virtually the same as those for the spiritual head. So it is with the Essene administrator. Besides managing the practical affairs of the assembly, he had to "instruct the multitudes concerning the works of God and to relate before them the great deeds of past times." He was enjoined "to love them as a father his children and as a shepherd his flock."

Such a delegation of service accounts for leadership in two of the three major departments of any social organization, namely, the spiritual-cultural and the administrative. But there is a third, the judiciary. In the Essene community those serving in this third sphere required more than a knowledge of jurisprudence. They had to be versed in the statutes of the Covenant—the New Covenant, of which the Essenes regarded themselves as the representatives—and in spiritual as well as civil law. Thus, this esoteric society organized its social body, not after some theoretical academic concept or chance arrangement, but scientifically in accordance with the threefold constitution of man himself. Here is the basic formula that every nation and people will ultimately adopt when the present systems of government have proven their inadequacy for securing freedom, justice and equality for all. The Essenes enjoyed such a state because they possessed the key to the type of social order that could provide it.

The Covenanters, to use a term Millar Burrows favors in designating members of the Dead Sea Community, discharged their social obligations to the larger community of which they formed only a section. They worked with others but after working hours returned to their own communal abodes. They performed all kinds of labor, entered into the various contemporary occupations and professions except those in any way directly related to forces of destruction or to promoting self-interest at the expense of others. Hence, they took no part in making instruments of war or implements devised for the destruction of life—human or subhuman. They revered life as a gift of God, a gift no man could bestow and, therefore, had no right to destroy unnecessarily.

Nor did they engage in commercial activities wherein the profit motive entered; they procured their necessities through simple barter. They avoided every activity and association that by their very nature tended to strengthen the proclivities of "natural man" at the expense of spiritual man. Their goal was to realize an impersonal, selfless life and a consciousness of universal amity based on the brotherhood of man under the fatherhood of God.

Two Groups—The Marrying and the Non—Marrying

The Essene Community was divided into two principal groups, the marrying and the non-marrying. The former established homes and sought to govern themselves in accordance with the Order's emphasis on living chaste and holy lives. They also adopted orphans whom they brought up to serve their Society. Non-marrying members, the innermost esoteric group, had taken the vow of celibacy. In their accounts about the Essenes this group receives the most attention from contemporary observers.

"These Initiate brethren," writes Corinne Heline in *New Age Bible Interpretation, Vol. IV*, "were taught the Mysteries of the Fire-Mist in the human body—its nature, its origin and the way of its ascent to the head, there to be used in various kinds of mental-spiritual creative activity and to stimulate the functions of the pineal and pituitary glands whose awakening makes man more than man. The presence of these two spiritual organs in the head was known to ancient Initiates, as references to them are still to be found in the writings of the Church Father Hippolytus, who, not being himself a believer in the Mysteries, was always attempting to discredit them. He nevertheless has done the service of preserving an ancient description of the organs in the head which, as he states, were likened to organs of generation, the head itself being likened to a marriage chamber. There in the brain the Serpent Fire has its true home, but descends by way of the medulla oblongata through the spine to the lower organs of physical generation. Modern anatomists know that the pituitary body in particular has an intimate connection with the sex function, and occult anatomists know that it has an equally intimate connection with regeneration and the fruition of spiritual powers."

Consider the foregoing in conjunction with a further development of the subject as presented by Mrs. Heline in her brochure, *The Immaculate Conception*, the second in her series of twelve booklets on *Occult Anatomy and the Bible*, "Every human being after puberty," she states, "during the monthly moon cycle of twenty-eight days, develops within himself a sacred seed which is formed of divine creative brain substance. This work is completed each month as the Moon enters the sign which the Sun occupied at birth ... The Temple Initiates who had taken the vow of perpetual virginity were taught how to lift this seed to the head and thus illumine the spiritual organs, the pituitary and pineal glands, and to make its forces available in various forms of mental and spiritual creative activities."

The lunar cycle in relation to human life, and especially in the development of the higher spiritual faculties, underlay that other important doctrine and practice among the Essenes which had to do with carefully and faithfully observing certain times and seasons, including "the circuits of the moon," as the *Manual* literally expresses it.

Closely associated with the foregoing subject is the practice of observing quiet, thoughtful speech and periods of silence. The Essenes did so for the conservation of the sacred life force at two creative centers in the body of man, one at the base of the spine and the other at its summit. The reason the innermost circle of the Sons of Truth made themselves "eunuchs for the kingdom of heaven's sake," to quote an utterance of the Master, was also their reason for disciplining their speech to "communications by Yea,yea; Nay, nay," to again quote Christ Jesus. In other words, conversation was limited to what had meaning and purpose. Both disciplines were observed to conserve sacred energies for use in serving God and man.

That there is a close connection between the sacral and the throat centers is generally recognized. One familiar manifestation of this relationship is the change of voice that occurs in boys upon reaching the age of puberty. Spiritual science teaches that the present mode of physical reproduction, which began when humanity was divided into sexes, will pass when mankind again attains an androgynous state. The "Lost Word" will then be found again, and man will reproduce his kind by speaking the creative word. "God said" and it was so. Ages hence it will be recorded, "Man said" and it was so. Such a development is already present in embryo.

One of the added powers acquired by sublimation of physical energies into those of the spirit is ability to heal, even to exorcising obsessing evil entities. The Essenes, as already mentioned, were distinguished for healing practices, by which they effected apparently miraculous cures. They were "good Samaritans." They pioneered in welfare work. When they set up camps or established centers of activity they fixed upon a place to which the needy and afflicted could come for help and healing. These stations were like clinics and later developed into hospitals such as we have today.

Wherever there is true spiritual development there is inner light for teaching and inner power for healing Preach the gospel and heal the sick—such was the command Christ gave to disciples He had empowered with divine gifts for doing both. So long as the Mystery Wisdom governed the early Church, it fulfilled both functions. And so it was among the forerunners who constituted the "Assembly of God," a term by which the Essenes were also known.

The Essenes investigated the subtle properties in minerals and plants and drew upon these in their healing ministry Desert dwellers that they were, they entered into an understanding communion with the inner or life side of nature, such a communion as is possible only in the quiet and relatively uncontaminated physical and psychical atmosphere of the wide open spaces.

Essenism, Freemasonry and Rosicrucianism

Under magnificent and elaborate symbolism and ritual, Free masonry has preserved in external form the Initiate Wisdom of old. The spiritual truths veiled by their outer forms—truths now almost forgotten and unrecognized—were alive and active among the Essenes, who were rightly known as Sons of Truth, possessors of the divine Gnosis.

Freemasonry bears witness to the fact by associating this pre-Christian community of true universalists with the first of the Philosophic Degrees of the Ancient and Accepted Scottish Rite. In the classification of grades the first of two degrees belonging to the Fourth Series are described as the "Apocalyptic and Christian Grades" and the seventeenth of the thirty-three degrees is called "Knights of the East and West." The master is styled *Venerable* and represents John the Baptist. The lodge room is in the shape of a heptagon. In each of the seven corners is a square column, at the top and bottom of which is inscribed a virtue to be cultivated. In the center of the room is a lamb lying on a book bearing seven seals and the names of the seven churches.

This pattern relates to the numerical power governing the manifestation of the Eternal through time. The universal operation of these sevenfold cycles of growth was as well understood by the Essenes as it is by those who are at all familiar with spiritual science. The number appears so frequently in Essenian writings that one scholar working on the *Scrolls* surmises it was evidently regarded as possessing some particular mystic significance.

And so it does.

The wisdom the Essenes strove for was connected with the mystery of numbers. They followed a mystical path of forty-two (6 x 7) clearly defined degrees or steps. "Once these were passed," says Dr. Steiner, "the Essene knew he was freed from the influences of the world of sense, and had reached the point . . . where he felt the center of his being to be united with Divinity." After six cycles of seven comes the seventh, wherein everything attained in the six begins to function on a new plane of power, a new level of consciousness.

In this connection it may be noted that, according to the "book of generations" as given by Matthew in the opening chapter of his Gospel, there are forty-two generations from "Father Abraham" to "Jesus the Christ, the Son of God." The origin of the Gospel of Matthew is traced to the Essenes. Their Teacher instructed a pupil named Matthew in these matters, who in turn handed them down in direct line to the Matthew of the first Gospel.

The designation, "Knight of the East and the West," points to a philosophic system and an initiatory institution such as those developed by the Essenes in Palestine and the Therapeutae in Egypt. "In the creeds of these two sects," Albert Pike writes, "there is unmistakably an intermingling of oriental and occidental rites, of Persian and Pythagorean opinions."

This fact is accounted for by Dr. Steiner, "All the people who were united in the sects of the Therapeutae and Essenes were under a certain common spiritual guidance." Specifically, that guidance came from the Essenian Teacher of Righteousness. Albert Pike observes further that truths, imperishable as Deity and undeniable as light, taught in the schools of Alexandria and by the shores of the Dead Sea, also by John the Baptist in the desert, survive in Masonry. They were "truths" gathered by the Essenes from the doctrines of the Orient and the Occident, from the Zend-Avesta and the Vedas, from Plato and Pythagoras, from India, Persia, Phoenicia and Syria, from Greece and Egypt, and from the Holy Books of the Jews, hence we (Masons) are called Knights of the East and the West."

Enid Smith, in the Rosicrucian article previously referred to, makes the statement that "the Freemasons find pure Christianity in Essenism and consider the Brethren of the White Clothing, or the Mystic Order of Essenes, to be the most important fraternity the world has ever seen." Manly Hall makes an almost identical statement about another historically linked esoteric group, namely, the Ancient and Honorable Order of the Rose Cross. He states that this "Fama Fraternitatis," this Mystery School of the West, while functioning from no visible physical center and through no identifiable members, is, nevertheless, "the most important institution in the Western World." Hence it is not by chance but by natural affinity that the second of the two Masonic "Apocalypltic and Christian Grades" should be the "Knight of the Rose Croix."

What gives such importance to these two specific groupings of advanced, illumined souls, the Essene Brotherhood and the Invisible Order of the Brothers of the Rose Cross? Is it their allegiance to the Christ? Essenism was mystic Christianity. So, too, is Rosicrucianism. The Essenes constituted themselves into a collective unity to sustain and help propel the initial release of a spiritual impulse that came to the world with the Divine Incarnation. In the early thirteenth century, the Rosicrucian Fraternity founded a Mystery School in Europe to reinforce this Christ impulse, which by that time had lost much of its original dynamism and was in need of a powerful recharging. According to Dr. Steiner, the Essenes had "a clear vision of man's path to a divine Being who had not yet descended into matter," while *true* Rosicrucianism (there is not a little that is *pseudo*) is dedicated to the task of helping mankind find its way to the resurrected Christ.

We have said the Essenes came at a time when one age was giving way to another, when an Old Dispensation was being superseded by the New. They were a part of both. They were strict adherents to the Law of Moses; they lived the Love of Christ. This same coupling is basic to Rosicrucianism. The founder of the latter esoteric movement bore the symbolic name of Christian Rose-Cross. When his physical body was discovered long after his passing there were found on its breast copies of both Testaments of the Christian Bible. On one side was the Law and the Prophets; on the other, the Gospel of Love. Christianity does not discard the Hebrew Scriptures, nor any other pre-Christian Bible; instead it fulfills them. Into historical continuity it injects a new beginning.

In amplification of the foregoing, Dupont-Sommer calls attention to how tenets and ideals of the two were woven into the life and consciousness of the Essenes. Says he, "The Gospel of forgiveness is all through the Testaments (Testaments of the Twelve Patriarchs); and there occurs here the first known conjunction—which was to be repeated in Mark 12:19-31—of the precept of Deuteronomy 6:5 to 'love the Lord thy God with all thy heart,' etc., and that of Leviticus 19:18 to 'love thy neighbor as thyself.' The injunction to love one's neighbor or brother turns up also in the *Book of Jubilees* and the Zadokite fragments."

In *New Age Bible Interpretation*, Vol. IV, Corrine Heline

describes their most salient qualities of character and disp sition as peace-loving, brotherly mindedness, being virtuously disposed toward others, selflessness in service, complete dedication to all that is high and holy. To quote in part, "They made no instrument of war and repudiated every inducement to covetousness. There were no slaves, but all were free, equal and served each other. They were instructed in piety, holiness, righteousness and economy; guided by a threefold rule—love of God, love of mankind and love of virtue. Their love of God was manifested beautifully in their constant and unalterable holiness of life. Their love of virtue showed itself in their indifference to money, fame and pleasure; also in their life of chastity, simplicity and modesty. Their love of man was exemplified in benevolence, equality, reverence and the care of the aged . . . Strangers were always welcomed as brothers without money and without price. All living things were to them a part of God's life and therefore sacred. It was their highest ideal to become fit temples for the Holy Ghost . . .and worthy forerunners of the Messiah. They taught humility and purity as the chief virtues and they lived in retirement from the world.

"They regarded the body as the soul's prison house and sought trials and difficulties rejoicingly for they had learned that 'wisdom is crystallized pain.' They gloried in martyrdom, preaching and singing to God even in their sufferings. They not only forgave their enemies but sought to benefit them and blessed even the criminals despite their destruction of life and property . . . The teaching held paramount was complete control of all passion and emotion, and its importance was stressed from the very beginning even in the training of the youngest neophytes. The habitual garment was the flowing white robe of linen such as worn by the Master when He came to John for baptism."

PART THREE

FORERUNNERS–PAST AND PRESENT

The Teacher of Righteousness

bout a hundred years before the advent of Christ the Essenes came under the inspiration and direction of an illumined individual to whom they referred as the Teacher of Righteousness. His name, like that of Yaveh among the Hebrews, was regarded as unpronounceable. In such high veneration did they hold him. As already mentioned, they also referred to him by various other titles such as the Master of Justice, the Elect of God, the Unique Founder, the Law Giver and the Anointed One. The last indicates that by the Essencs he was regarded as fulfilling a messianic mission.

The Teacher was a seer of lofty rank, a preserver of wisdom from the past and a prophet of things to come. He spoke prophetically of the Christ as "the Lion who was to come forth from the line of David." Reference here is to the Sun Spirit, a lion being the pictorial symbol of Leo, the zodiacal sheath of the Sun. It was another form of Zoroaster's prophecy that Ahura Mazda, the radiant Sun Spirit was drawing nearer the earth and would in the fullness of time enter upon a human incarnation.

The teachings and the way of life proclaimed and demonstrated by the Teacher of Righteousness were so far in advance of those followed by conventional religionists of the time that he incurred opposition from the official priesthood in

Jerusalem. Charging him with blasphemy and heresy, its leaders not only rejected his message but subjected him to indignities and persecution before finally condemning him to death. He was stoned and then hung upon a cross, thus adding disgrace to punishment. He is said to have suffered "in his body of flesh," a phrase evidently implying the belief that he was a divine messenger who had taken human form. He was, in fact, a prototype of Christ Jesus, for whose coming he was preparing the way.

As stated, the Essenes developed out of Judaism but differed from its orthodoxy in their doctrines and practices. They were equally out of harmony with the political institutions under which they lived since religion and statecraft of that time were closely united. Hence, they were subject to persecution from members of the prevailing religious and political parties.

Historical Setting

The Essenes functioned during the era in Palestinian history known as the Maccabean Period. It extended from 164 to 40 B.C., spanning the lifetime of the Teacher of Righteousness. The Maccabees were an heroic family that delivered Judea and Judaism from the persecutions of the Syrian King, Antiochus Epiphanes, and later established a dynasty of priest-kings which proved to be antagonistic to the Essenes and their leader. The Maccabeans were originally known as the Hasmoneans, a name also applied to this period of Palestinian history.

Aristobulus I, son of John Hyrcanus, ruled as king of Judea from 105 to 104 B.C. He is said to have been the first of the Hasmoneans to assume that title. Aristobulus I was succeeded by Alexander Jannaeus who assumed the double role of priest-king (104-78 B.C.). Then followed the rulership by two brothers, Aristobulus II and Hyrcanus II. They were the last priest-kings of Jerusalem and their leadership, together with Judean independence, came to an end when the Romans under Pompey entered Jerusalem in 63 B.C. and took Aristobulus II as captive to Rome.

Professor Dupont-Sommer believes these last two Maccabean priests were responsible for the condemnation and death of the Teacher of Righteousness. He identifies them as the "Prophets of Untruth," the "Wicked Priests" and "Persecutors of the Elect" referred to in the Essenian *Commentary on the Book of Habakkuk*. Aristobulus II is singled out as "the enemy who beguiled many" and whose "shame exceeded his glory."

Professor Allegro gives it as his opinion that the tragedy occurred earlier; that it was Alexander Jannaeus who, early in the first century B.C., descended on the Essene community by the Dead Sea and seized the Teacher as he was offering sacrifice at the altar. "As now seems possible from a recently discovered manuscript," this authority states, "he then gave him into the hands of his Gentile mercenaries to be crucified. Then after the tyrant had left the scene, the scattered disciples returned and reverently buried the body of their Teacher in a tomb near by, where they settled down in the way of life ordained for them, to await his glorious return as Messiah of God."

In addition to the information about the Teacher of Righteousness contained in the *Habakkuk Commentary*, there are references to him in the *Manual of Discipline* and the earlier discovered *Damascus Document*. In both of these manuscripts followers of the Prophet are described as members of a New Covenant.

Jesus ben Pandira

Who was this Teacher of Righteousness? Who was this inspired Master who figures so prominently in writings of the Essenes but was never mentioned by name? Identification based on historical documents have not solved the mystery conclusively. There is no doubt about the existence of a very remarkable individual who lived among those making up the Dead Sea Community. The problem of his identification is complicated, however, by the fact that there were two extraordinary persons who appeared on the scene in Palestine while the Essenes functioned as an organized movement. Not

67

only were there two spiritual luminaries in their midst, but both bore the name of Jesus. Yet the full names by which they entered into historical records distinguishes them, the one being known as Jesus ben Pandira—that is, Jesus the son of Pandira—and the other, Jesus of Nazareth.

This distinction cannot be accepted as proof positive that the two names do not belong to one and the same personage. What tends to overrule the difference in appellation is the similarity of their lives. According to historical accounts both were luminous souls, both were held in reverent awe by their followers, both were condemned to death by their enemies for nonconformity to the established order and popular beliefs. Supernatural incidents accompanied their birth; they went for a time into Egypt, and both were acknowledged as teachers with great influence and possessing powers whereby to perform miraculous healings.

In addition to the foregoing it must be admitted that outside Gospel narratives information about Jesus of Nazareth is very scant, and even these have been seriously challenged as to their authenticity. Hence, to those who look upon the Gospels as non-historical presentations of major steps on the Path of Initiation—as set forth in Mystery Teachings throughout the ages—it is not strange that skeptical researchers, who base their conclusions on historical documents, question whether Jesus of Nazareth is the Jesus whose name appears in rabbinical writings of a much earlier date than that ascribed to the Master of Galilee.

G.R.S. Meade, author of *Pistis Sophia*, a Gnostic Gospel, and other erudite occult works, has written a whole book on the subject, titled *Did Jesus Live 100 Years B.C.?* A number of occult writers have answered this question in the affirmative. Charles Leadbeater, for example, in his work on *The Hidden Side of Christian Festivals*, gives 105 B.C. as the birth year of Jesus of Nazareth. Others have fixed his birth at about 115 B.C. But this was not the Jesus of the Gospels. It was Jesus of the Talmud, Jesus ben Pandira. Because this earlier Jesus did live a life bearing an initiatory character, some students of comparative religion have concluded that he was taken as a pattern by Gospel writers for their delineation of major events universally experienced by all who enter the Path that leads to Illumination. This apparently well-founded disposal of Jesus of Nazareth gives added credence to the position they take on the historicity of the Gospel story. The latter is accepted only as a symbolized presentation of the great reality that Divine Incarnation is a spiritual fact and a universal truth, but that it should not be understood as having taken place in physical human form. According to this interpretation the Lord did not literally take on flesh and dwell among men; a Divine Incarnation there was, and is, but they maintain, only in a mystical sense and as it occurs in humanity at large, and as it manifests as light and power in awakened, developed souls.

That this is one aspect of the Christ incarnation is agreed by the orthodox church and Rosicrucian Christianity. But the Christology of these widely separated groups is equally emphatic in teaching that the Christ spirit entered into a human personality, into the body of Jesus of Nazareth, in a unique manner; and that in Christ Jesus, a divinized human, a God-man actually walked the earth.

The only difference between orthodoxy and Rosicrucianism regarding the Divine Incarnation is that the former believe this to have occurred at the time of the birth of Jesus while the latter teach that the conjunction between the human and the divine did not take place until the baptism of Jesus by John. Only after that event, according to the esoteric interpretation, did Jesus become Christed. Only then began the three-year ministry which the Gospels record, a ministry which continued until the release of the Christ spirit at the time of the crucifixion on Golgotha.

In the life, death and resurrection of Christ Jesus, all that had previously been enacted prophetically in the Ancient Mysteries as ritualistic drama occurred in the life of this God-man. In His being was embodied the content of what earlier hierophants had foreseen and portrayed with consistent similarity in their Schools of Initiation. "Myth" became history. Students of

69

comparative religion too often fail to distinguish between the two. Since ancient mythology is not to be taken literally, whatever took an identical form in history is dismissed as myth.

Orthodoxy, like esoteric Christianity, affirms the doctrine of the historical, physical incarnation of the Christos. But having rejected the reliability and authenticity of wisdom available through spiritual science, it lacks an interpretation that commends itself to the skeptical, rationalistic mind of modern man. Esoteric Christianity, however, draws upon the Mystery Wisdom where it finds a whole body of fact into which it can rationally place that unique, composite Being whose chain of vehicles or principles extends from man to God and whom we know as Christ Jesus.

To both schools of Christianity it is a matter of very real importance that the historicity of Jesus of Nazareth be firmly established. He is not to be evaporated into a mere image nor to be confused with a personage who lived a century earlier. There is room in history and in theology for both image and object; for Jesus of the Talmud and Jesus of the Gospels. Jesus ben Pandira was the most luminous among saintly souls congregated in Palestine to prepare for Jesus of Nazareth, who was to become the bearer of the Christ; he was, in fact, a prototype of the Galilean Master, but he was not Jesus of the Gospels.

Research on the basis of historical documents alone has not brought forth sufficient evidence to solve the enigma among academic scholars as to the identity of the Essene Teacher of Righteousness and whether or not Jesus ben Pandira and Jesus of Nazareth are the same or are two different personalities. Fortunately, there are other chronicles to be consulted by those who have acquired ability to read them. Dr. Rudolf Steiner was an investigator possessing such ability. He was a trained scientific observer capable of reading in the Memory of Nature, and the subject in question came quite fully within his vast esoteric purview. Some results of his researches are to be found in two of his volumes: *From Jesus to Christ* and *The Gospel of St. Matthew*. Also in two lectures he delivered in Leipzig, Nov. 4th and 5th, 1911.

For those who can accept the validity of Dr. Steiner's inner-plane investigations, speculation gives way to scientific knowledge. The simple facts emerging from his occult inquiry identify the Essene Teacher of Righteousness with Jesus ben Pandira, who lived about a hundred years B.C. His name appears in rabbinical literature, sometimes spelled Jesu ben Pandira and also Jeshua ben Pandira. The Talmud, like other Jewish writings, presents a picture of this Adept that is, in the words of Dr. Steiner, "either misleading or deliberately falsified." All that is told about him is, he says, "calumny."

To follow Dr. Steiner's exposition, Jesus ben Pandira was a highly evolved ego that had attained to the status of a Bodhisattva. This is a Hindu term. As used in Buddhism it denotes one who has entered the path of Buddhahood and will, generally in a future incarnation, become a Buddha. It is to be remembered that *Buddha* is not the name of an individual but designates a rank of honor.

Prior to the elevation of Jesus ben Pandira to the rank of a Bodhisattva, this office had been filled by Prince Gautama, son of King Saddhodana, over a period of many, many lives before he attained to Buddhahood. This promotion of the Indian prince to the status of a Buddha occurred in his twenty-ninth year, while in profound meditation under the Bodhi tree, the "tree of knowledge." It was an experience comparable in a certain sense, though not identical, to what occurred to Jesus at the time of his baptism by John. Then it was that Jesus in his egoic being made a voluntary surrender of his earthly vehicles to the Christ, that in and through a human form the latter might manifest the works of God and prepare a secure foundation on which a new and redeemed humanity could arise.

Dr. Steiner tells us that since his assumption of the office of a Bodhisattva after it was vacated by prince Gautama in the sixth century B.C., he who bore the name of Jesus ben Pandira has reincarnated in almost every century for the purpose of helping humanity in some important way in connection with its on-going. Also that he is in incarnation today—or was at the time Dr. Steiner made the statement some forty years ago. After more lives of service to humanity in the capacity of a Bodhisattva, Jesus ben Pandira, the Essene Teacher of Righteousness, will rise to the exalted estate of that one whom the ancients foresaw as the Buddha Maitreya, the Bringer of Good, the Bearer of spiritual powers having saving potencies.

It was Jesus ben Pandira who, together with his Essene followers, heralded the coming to this earth plane of the Lord Christ, the promised Messiah; and he will again be the real herald of the return of Christ, not this time in a physical body but in His etheric raiment. On His first coming the Christ had to descend all the way to the physical plane to manifest His glory and power before men and to overcome the powers of materiality and death. On His second coming He will not need to descend lower than the etheric plane. What He did at the time of His human incarnation has given humanity power to meet Him part way up the ladder that extends from densest matter to pure spirit. We will be able to meet "the Lord in the air," as Paul expressed it, or on etheric levels.

To proclaim the form in which the Christ would appear on His first and also on His second coming was one of the tasks assigned to Jesus ben Pandira at the time he assumed the role of a Bodhisattva. Again quoting Dr. Steiner, "He has the mission of directing men's eyes more and more to that which man can love, to bring it about that what men can spread abroad as a theory shall flow into a moral channel, so that at length all that men can possess in the form of thoughts shall stream into the moral life."

Preparation for Christ's First and Second Coming

From the foregoing we are given to understand that Jesus ben Pandira is again active in the world, helping to prepare humanity for receiving its King of Glory on His second coming. Generally speaking, the souls that gathered to make preparation for Christ's first advent have reassembled in our time to create world conditions suitable to His reappearance.

While the need for such preparation is apparently no less

today than it was two thousand years ago, the mode and manner of meeting it is quite different. For one thing, retirement from the world and an ascetic way of life were essential to ancient forerunners of Christ in order to properly condition themselves for effectively fulfilling their mission. This is no longer so. On the contrary, forerunners of today must participate actively in the affairs of this world and project their spiritual idealism not only into the religious field but also into the spheres of politics, business, education, the arts and every other phase of everyday living. They must be able to uphold spiritual faith and vision in the midst of the din and pressures of the market place, not solely from the peaceful, secluded atmosphere of sanctified retreats. They must mingle in world affairs, working creatively on objective as well as subjective levels. Only thus can the world community, which has now been knit into a global unity, be prepared for the coming world event of Christ's reappearance.

There is another difference. The compact little community in ancient Palestine came under the immediate tutelage of a single Master mind. Today the wide and varied composition of the company of souls which is now preparing for Christ's second coming look to different leaders for instruction, guidance and inspiration. There is no single, divinely commissioned leader corresponding to the Essenian Teacher of Righteousness to direct the world-wide company of this day. Moreover, external direction is no longer required to the same degree that it was in former times. It now comes increasingly from within man's own soul. Man changes "with the processes of the Suns." He grows. His spiritual faculties come into greater maturity. And so "the time in man's evolution has passed," writes Dr. Steiner, "when human beings were led by the Gods from above, from the Higher Worlds. In ever increasing measure men will have to do things for themselves without being directed and led."

When the Christ first appeared the world to which He could immediately address Himself was relatively small. So, too, was the community of forerunners. It is otherwise today. The world to which the returning Christ will immediately address Himself will be global. So, too, will be the community of forerunners. It will be

73

composed of divinely oriented souls regardless of differing theological convictions and religious affiliations. They will be drawn from every walk of life and from all lands; they will constitute no formally organized body and will be largely unknown to each other personally. Yet they will be subjectively linked in their polarization toward the Christ and in their common efforts of preparing for the reappearance of the Teacher of Angels and men, the Saviour of the World.

Reintroducing the Ancient Wisdom

Such souls are being drawn together. It is one of the major spiritual developments of this present period. It may be dated as commencing on a broad scale in the last quarter of the nineteenth century with the founding of the Theosophical Society. This represented an organized effort to reintroduce the general public to the Ancient Wisdom that for centuries past has been in virtual obscuration. It was designed to promote a universal religion and to work for the brotherhood of man under the Fatherhood of God. This program is absolutely basic to creating conditions, not only propitious but essential to the remanifestation of the Christed Glory Light.

Following the magnificent pioneering work done by the Theosophists during the latter part of the nineteenth century and on up to the present time—the driving of a wedge into a scientific materialism that had come to dominate our civilization and through which the liberalizing and redeeming forces of spiritual science had to percolate—there appeared the various Rosicrucian organizations. These came at the turn of the century to greatly amplify the work initiated by the Theosophists by developing that aspect of the Ancient Wisdom which embodies the Mysteries of Christos; for, as previously stated, Rosicrucianism *is* Mystic Christianity.

In the voluminous writings of the occult scientist, Rudolf Steiner, and those of the Christian mystic, Max Heindel, the modern seeker after spiritual realities is given clear and emphatic direction for finding the Christ. The whole of their works has for

74

its supreme aim the leading of humanity into an understanding of the Christ in His historical, planetary, cosmic and mystical aspects. This is also the distinctive feature of Corinne Heline's *New Age Bible Interpretation*. The Christ theme permeates its pages from Genesis to Revelation. It is the theme that most needs emphasis in our time. A greater awakening and cultivation of the Christ consciousness are necessary preludes to the return of the World Redeemer. Not until such spiritual awakening and development reach sufficient strength to provide the required "atmosphere" can the Christ do for humanity what is so desperately needed, and for which it consciously and unconsciously longs and prays.

The teachings that have been given out in the past few decades by the Theosophical and Rosicrucian schools, together with those of many related occult and mystical bodies in all parts of the world, have come to constitute a vast and comprehensive body of spiritual science. The very reason for the release of this science and its promulgation in various and diverse ways, here, there and everywhere, is to prepare the world for again receiving her spiritual King, the Lord Christ. *"In order to prepare for this event,"* declares Dr. Steiner, *"spiritual science exists, and every one who works at cultivating and spreading this wisdom shares in making this preparation."*

Paul Brunton states virtually the same thing in an article on *Science and Spiritual Knowledge* in *The Ananai*, a Japanese magazine of January, 1957. He writes of the useful and necessary contribution science has made in promoting intellectual development and in improving our physical surroundings, but that this has all been done in ignorance of spiritual laws governing mankind; that this lack has brought about disastrous results, so it has now become imperative for mankind's safety and progress to extend the boundaries of physical science to include spiritual science. Such Knowledge, he adds, is available, and it is the destiny of man to acquire and live by it. *"Only when that destiny is fulfilled,"* he concludes significantly, *"will it be possible for a Savior's voice to make itself sufficiently heard."*

Among the many groups within the field of spiritual science is one called *The Christian Community*. It was inspired by teachings of Dr. Steiner and first came into operation in England in 1923. It is centered in the Christian Mysteries. It retains the holy sacraments, which it observes with an understanding of their esoteric significance and in the same reverential spirit as that in which the Essenes performed their ritual ablutions and sacramental communal meals. It is a small community by present quantitative measurements. So was the Essene Brotherhood. But this is not the measure of worth of such pioneering movements. It is the depth of dedication that counts. Their value lies in their proclaiming the truths most needed at this time, and their vital connection with the forces of growth and the creative powers of spirit to be released into the world. They are seed-bearers. The seeds planted may be small but the promise they hold is bounteous. It is values such as these that gave to the little Essene Community the transforming power which history bears witness. It is similar values that give significance to various modern movements of which the *Christian Community* is an inspiring example.

Another movement that is specifically dedicated to the task of building the kind of world and encouraging the type of consciousness to which the Christ can make His reappearance is *The Group of World Servers*. This group constitutes an outwardly scattered body but an inwardly linked community of self-directed individuals who have acquired inner strength and perception—aided, to be sure, by those who stand above and go before—to respond to spiritual demands of the times and to serve them with intelligence, judgment and effectiveness.

The members are on no roster and subscribe to no specified doctrinal beliefs or practices. Their common bond is dedication to world service and the conditioning of human consciousness for the reception of the Christ Impulse into their lives, and through them into the world at large as preparatory to His reapearance and a new outpouring of His spirit on all mankind. Those comprising the

Group of World Servers are drawn from any and every race and country, from people both inside and outside the spheres of organized religion.

This movement was intiated by The Tibetan, also known as the Master Dwal Khul who, through the channelship of Alice A. Bailey, has made a major contribution to current esoteric literature. Among the many volumes he has authored is one most emphatically addressed to the present historic moment; it is titled *The Reappearance of Christ*. The title itself is highly significant. Linked as it is to the activity of the World Servers it further emphasizes the fact that today a global community is preparing for the world reappearance of our planetary Redeemer. This becomes yet more manifest in connection with the fact that the Tibetan is an oriental; he belongs to a Buddhist country and presides over a Himalayan Lamasery. But is the higher light of Mystery Wisdom there affiliations and allegiances are not inconsistent with his acknowledgement of the Christ as Head of the directing Hierarchy of our planetary life and the supreme Light of the World, for whose reappearance we must prepare.

As the Christ on His return will speak, not only to those who bear His name but to all the peoples of the world, so His coming will be attended, not by a small localized group as it was in Palestine two thousand years ago but by a world-wide Church Universal. Awakened souls could ask no greater privilege than that of participating consciously, as did the Essenes of old, in clearing the way for this glorious event.

The Appointed Time

The Essenes were living in "the latter days"—the latter days of the Old Dispensation. As such they were days of judgment. Upon the unfaithful in Israel who held to the letter of the law, the "letter that killeth," who waxed rich at the expense of the poor and who persecuted those who came bringing true light, there descended calamities of invasion and plunder by the Romans, along with the loss of freedom and independence. According to Josephus, the store of gold amassed by the last rulers of Israel was

77

so great he felt it necessary to explain at length how such great sums had come into their hands.

This judgment upon Israel commenced with Pompey's invasion in 63 B.C.; then with the capture of Jerusalem by Herod the Great in 37 B.C.; and again when the city fell to the Romans under Titus in 67 A.D. The judgment, according to the *Habakkuk Commentary*, was "for a fixed time," a time "of the end." It states further that "the final time will be of long duration, and it will exceed all that the prophets had said; for the Mysteries of God will be marvelous."

The "final time" extended over a century. "But if it delays," wrote the prophet, "wait for it; for it will be sure to come and it will not be late." To this the Essenian commentator adds, "This refers to the men of truth who practiced the law, whose hands do not relax in the service of truth when the final time is delayed for them; for all the times of God arrive in due season in accordance with what He had decreed about them in the Mysteries of His Prudence." Hence, the admonition to the faithful "to persevere, to retain an absolute confidence, to remain firmly attached to the truth."

The foregoing is pertinent to the present generation which is also living in "the latter days"—the latter days of another age—when divine judgment is again being meted out to the nations. For the past half-century that judgment has been dispensed in shattering events of planetary proportions. Another half-century may not be too long a time for order and equilibrium to be restored to the world. It is even now as it was when the Old Dispensation was giving way to the New. In the present transition the trials, sorrow and suffering of the Piscean Age are gradually giving way to the brightness and brotherhood of the Age of Aquarius. As the world had to be conditioned for the first coming of Christ, so it must be reconditioned for His second coming.

While there is truth in the statement that there is an eternal recurrence of the identical, it is only true if the identical is understood as a repetition of similar processes and procedures at corresponding points on an ever-ascending spiral of becoming. This is the truth underlying a folk-wisdom that found expression in the saying that "the more things change, the more they remain the same."

All of which points to the fact that now is the "appointed time" for the discovery of ancient scrolls containing a message as important to the present generation as it was to the generation to which it was addressed two thousand years ago. Today, as then, the call is to stand steady and remain serene in the midst of turmoil, distress and change, and to make straight the way for the coming Light of the World.